Boris Fotografias Modernas
S. Paulo

JORGE AMERICANO, Professor of Law at the University of Sao Paulo, started his career as a clerk in the Finance Ministry while still a student of law in Sao Paulo. He was a public attorney in the interior, 1915-1918, a lawyer in Sao Paulo and Santos, 1918-1928, and general attorney in Rio de Janeiro, 1928-1930. Since then he has taught law at the University, acting as Dean of the Law School in 1939, and serving a five-year term as President of the University, 1941-1946.

Dr. Americano is the author of many books in Portuguese on legal and sociological subjects. He has traveled and lectured in Europe, Canada, and the United States, and his hobbies are chess and sailing.

THE NEW FOUNDATION OF
INTERNATIONAL LAW

THE MACMILLAN COMPANY
NEW YORK · BOSTON · CHICAGO
DALLAS · ATLANTA · SAN FRANCISCO

MACMILLAN AND CO., LIMITED
LONDON · BOMBAY · CALCUTTA
MADRAS · MELBOURNE

**THE MACMILLAN COMPANY
OF CANADA, LIMITED**
TORONTO

THE NEW FOUNDATION
OF
INTERNATIONAL LAW

BY JORGE AMERICANO

BRAZILIAN REPRESENTATIVE ON THE PERMANENT COURT OF
ARBITRATION; PROFESSOR OF LAW, UNIVERSITY OF
SÃO PAULO, BRAZIL

THE MACMILLAN COMPANY · NEW YORK
1947

FOREWORD TO THE AMERICAN EDITION

SOME of my friends who have read the Brazilian edition of this book, and concurred in the views stated in it, have expressed doubt that education could, within a few years, achieve the goal I have set for it to bring about world government.

To those who may doubt the practicality of achieving that goal, I point out the advances which have been made but recently in this field.

It is encouraging to consider the success of two important books, "The Anatomy of Peace" by Emery Reves and "Modern Man Is Obsolete" by Norman Cousins, and it is pleasantly surprising that the field of international policy, previously ignored by scientists, is now a matter of concern both to jurists and to scientists. We find together, in the same company, former United States Supreme Court Justice Owen J. Roberts, Senators J. William Fulbright, Claude D. Pepper, Elbert D. Thomas, Glen H. Taylor, Bishop Henry St. George Tucker, Edward A. Conway, Louis Finkelstein, Mortimer J. Adler, Charles G. Bolte, Gardner Cowles, Jr., Albert Einstein, Dorothy Canfield Fisher, Albert D. Lasker, Thomas Mann, Lieutenant Cord Meyer, Jr., Christopher Morley, Carl Van Doren, Walter Wanger, Robert J. Watt, Raymond Gram Swing, Carlos P. Romulo, Harry A. Overstreet, Niels Bohr, Arthur H. Compton, General Henry H. Arnold, Hans Bethe, Edward U. Condon, Irving Langmuir, Walter Lippmann, Philip Morrison, J. R. Oppenheimer, Louis N. Ridenour, Jr., Frederick Seitz, Harlow Shapley, Leo Szilard, Harold C. Urey, Eugene P. Wigner, Gale Young.

The Conservative Anthony Eden and the Laborite Ernest Bevin agree upon a world government, and Winston Churchill more cautiously advances only as far as the idea of the European Confederation. That, too, would be an advance.

But as a matter of fact the ground has been prepared, and the decision rests with a few hundred persons all over the world—the professors of international law.

If—instead of basing their instruction on an overemphasized sovereignty, on the old concepts of war as a relation to be stated under "rules of war," on neutrality toward belligerents as a duty for all nations—they would teach that morals should be the same under both domestic and international law, that war is a crime, that there should be a world organization with powers of control and coercion, based on democratic principles, and capable of applying a Bill of Rights to men all over the world, then the few hundred professors of international law could do the greatest work ever done. Every year some thousands of students would assimilate those ideas, and within a few years a strong international consciousness would be formed.

These students would become politicians, journalists, diplomats, economists, professors, educators, and the face of the world would be changed.

Until recently, the battle of ideas in the international field was fought on the ground of sentiment and reason. Sentiment has been poisoned by mystics, and simple reason has been confused by propaganda. A juridical and scientific study has never been made. Scientists in all categories can contribute to such a study, but it is primarily a job for professors of international law.

To these professors I appeal.

As Bertrand Russell says, the average man—in spite of some benefits of pension and life insurance that secure his old age and guarantee, in the economic sense, safety of his life—is fed up with the monotony of his existence. Days come and go, weeks, months and years come and go, and he has always the same tasks to perform. He goes to the plant in the morning and comes back home in the evening, and has no opportunity to develop his initiative, to win the admiration of his fellows, to have some adventure in life. The repression of his desires and feelings is contrary to the nature of a human being. Thus, so soon as the newspapers announce a distant and perhaps non-significant conflict at the frontier, he escapes from the reality of his daily routine by recalling subconsciously that he is a member of a large community, that now he has the opportunity of becoming a new and adventurous man, a free man, full of self-reliance, anxious for adventure.

This explains the psychosis of war as it affects the individual.

FOREWORD TO THE BRAZILIAN EDITION

AT THE present time every teacher of international law is asking himself whether it is right to teach his students a law which is a failure. It, therefore, seems an opportune moment to propose a fresh approach toward international law.

That is what we are going to try to do here.

To plumb the depths of this subject would demand more than we have; but what is lacking in profundity will be offset by timeliness, in this early post-war period.

The intense activity in international politics needs to be supported by research. To be useful this must embrace problems with an open mind and lay aside the preconceptions of conventional international law and of domestic or international political passion.

Law is a system of guarantees, based on principles of justice. When the guarantees are not based on just principles, they become means of oppression, a general reaction sets in, and the very guarantees disappear. Whenever equity is lacking in the application of the principles of justice, reactions are set up which, recurring, produce insecurity.

Law is a cohesive whole. Civil law, commercial law, social welfare law, procedural, administrative, judiciary law, and constitutional law are branches of law, constituting groups of organized principles for the security of life in its various aspects. These principles should be based on justice.

The organization of life consists essentially of giving mankind tranquillity in which to live economically, socially and spiritually.

This is the object of all branches of law, and it has been tolerably well achieved by the internal laws of each nation in peacetime, that is, so long as the need does not arise to appeal to higher principles—to international law.

Whenever this need arises, in order to insure peace among the nations so that men may be assured the right to work, think and believe, international law fails and war comes.

Why? Because international law lacks *an organization to guarantee it;* it lacks any *basis of principles of justice;* it is a system built up on moral principles different from individual morality, and there has been little *equity in its application,* so that disputes have been settled by force.

What is needed, therefore, is a reform of its foundations, basing it on justice, like all other branches of law. In the present anomalous situation we have international law pitted *against* the national law of each country. *Law against law!* Efficient organizations must be set up to enable international law to work properly. Men must be taught to solve international problems equitably.

Our study will thus be divided into three parts—systematization, organization and education. We shall deal with them, setting aside classical international law with its lack of a just basis, efficient organization and equitable application.

We shall be objective in our research, working from stable facts to the principle they indicate. We shall check the principles by the principles of justice, so as to formulate a system of law in harmony with the other branches of law.

Our study of an international organization will take as a starting point what has been already partly achieved—the Security Council, the International Assembly, the Court of International Justice—and we shall seek to define their ambit.

With a view to guiding education toward the practice of international equity, we shall assess current standards of values in international affairs through objective criticism of commonly held ideas on modern problems.

To make a complete draft of such a scheme is, of course, beyond our powers. But if what existed before has gone to pieces, we must begin afresh; and the way to begin is by preparing rough drafts.

Where are we to begin? Democratic culture, defended by the United Nations, now victorious over Nazi Germany and Fascist Italy, and soon to be victorious over Japan,* has already laid down some basic points for the new system of international law:

1. There is an international community, for which a scheme of organization was attempted in the formation of the League of Nations, and continued in the formation of the United Nations organization;

2. It is the duty of the international community to guarantee the dignity of man (as stated in the Atlantic Charter);

3. The idea of absolute sovereignty is incompatible with such a guarantee (repeated statements by the United Nations that the self-determination proclaimed by the Atlantic Charter is irreconcilable with totalitarian regimes);

4. War is a crime against world security (statements by the United Nations, who are at present acting as a world police, that those who were responsible for the war must be judged by international courts);

5. There can be no neutrality between war—a crime—and law. (Ruy Barbosa at the Buenos Aires Conference, 1915);

6. The international community should be organized on the same lines as the organization of municipal law in each country, especially as to the division of legislative, executive and judicial powers (Inter-American Conference of Lawyers, Rio de Janeiro, 1943; Dumbarton Oaks Conference, 1944).

* Written before the end of the war with Japan.

Is it possible to build up an equitable system on these bases?

Every jurist, with his habit of considering relationships from a systematic point of view, can perceive in these principles the possibility of defining the *object of international law,* studying the *persons,* their *property* and the *juridical facts* which go to make it up, subdividing international juridical facts into *legal* and *illegal* ones and distinguishing *criminal acts* as a special section of the latter, and also considering certain measures of *preventive guarantee, repression* and *reparation* which can be exercised by a police power of the international community. Every jurist sees, too, that the efficiency of the international organization depends on the structure of its component parts and the possibility of the effective exercise of their functions.

Such are the true foundations of any legal system.

CONTENTS

xiii

PART TWO

ORGANIZATION OF THE INTERNATIONAL COMMUNITY

Part One

SYSTEMATIZATION

THE OBJECT OF INTERNATIONAL LAW

HUMAN LIFE and activities are legally systematized in the domestic sphere by one set of principles, which constitutes the law of domestic relations, economic and non-economic relations, and another set for assuring the use of goods indispensable to life. This second set of principles is divided up into the *law of property*, which establishes man's direct relations to property, and the *law of liability*, which establishes these same relations in regard to reciprocity of action with other men for the attainment of property, so that human actions take on the character of goods, called incorporeal goods. A last set of principles results from the transitory nature of human life as compared with the permanence of goods, whether corporeal or incorporeal, and constitutes the *law of inheritance*.

From the orderly arrangement of such groups—*domestic relations, property, liability* and *inheritance*—we arrive at the fundamental principles of the *civil law*. These principles apply to *persons, goods* and *actions,* the last being divided into *legal* and *illegal actions* as they are useful or harmful to man.

Apart from the *civil law* system, we have a set of special principles for the better and more rapid utilization of certain consumer goods. This constitutes *commercial law* which, together with *civil law,* forms *private law*.

In a perfect society, the relation of one man to another would be assured by the private law system. Their lack of conformity to the pattern, however, demands *provisions for public order,* to guarantee *life, liberty, proportional usage of goods* and *the efficacy of wills*.

This set of provisions for public order constitutes *social welfare law,* which lays down rules for restoring the equilibrium of legal equality in view of perturbing economic inequalities, and *criminal law,* which defines the antisocial acts demanding special consideration by means of penalties.

Proper adjustment of the *provision for public order* to the system of private law calls for the establishment of appropriate *organizations,* the definition of the respective *functions* and the acquisition of *financial means.* These belong to *constitutional law, administrative law* and *budget law.*

Constitutional law, therefore, defines the organization of the *nation-community,* constituting it a *state-community.* It sets up the *essential* organs, defines their *functions,* their *object* (which in a word is the security of the human being), the *essential guarantees for this purpose* and the *essential guarantees for the existence of the state.* It is, therefore, made up of structural and functional rules, principles essential to human life and activities, and guarantees for the self-support and self-defense of the state itself.

Given the structural and functional rules of the state-nation, *administrative law* regulates its functioning by means of *administrative law,* properly so called, in the sphere of executive state relations, and by means of *judicial law* in the sphere of investigatory and restorative action in the face of violations. *Judicial law* sets in motion *civil and penal lawsuits* for the investigation of violations and the effecting of legal remedies, both in ordinary cases (*civil wrongs*) and in extraordinary cases (*crimes*).

The juridical framework indicated above exists with greater or lesser perfection within each nation.

But collisions occur between the juridical frameworks of different nations. When such collisions occur between systems of private law they are settled by *international private law.* When they occur between systems of public law (collisions of sovereignties) they should be settled by *international public law.*

In international private law discord arising from differences in private law of different countries is regulated by general principles and international conventions or treaties, and solutions are executed by the internal agencies of each nation. Disregard of fundamental principles on the part of a nation in its internal law, or injustice in their application, may turn the discord into international conflict.

In international public law the causes of discord have arisen hitherto from the fact that the limits of a state's security have been laid down by that state itself, which has exaggerated the bounds of its security, assumed the right to regulate economic order for its own benefit, to the detriment of other states, and allowed itself to deny the value of human personality.

A further cause of discordance in international law is the fact that, while there ought to be, in human society, a set of more or less just laws, guaranteed by the domestic laws of each nation, equity has been lacking in these; the state is magnified and international relations endangered.

In short, discord results from an exaggerated conception of the state and a lack of equity in the value attributed to human personality.

Up to the present time there has not been any means of intervention in the family of nations for the purpose of restoring equity in the internal affairs of each nation. Neither has there been any process for reducing state hypertrophy, nor any instrument of sanction with a valid, lasting structure, nor any efficient system of sanctions.

What is needed, therefore, is a revision of the whole groundwork of international law with a view to:

(*a*) defining the *superstate* and fixing its limits;

(*b*) defining and delimiting the sphere of action of *other persons in international law;*

(*c*) defining and regulating *property in international law;*

(*d*) defining and regulating *international juridical acts* and their effects on persons and property in international law;

(*e*) defining the *violations* of the fundamental principles of international law and the measures of security, prevention, repression and reparation.

All these constitute *substantive international law.*

(*f*) establishing the agencies of the *international superstate,* their *functions, budget resources* and *functioning* (organic international law, administrative international law, budget international law, international judiciary and procedural law).

By means of private law man has been able to regulate the principles of his life. By internal public law he has sought to create means of guaranteeing them. It still remains for external or international public law *to examine the equity of these principles and the structure and functioning of the agencies guaranteeing domestic public law, to define a superstate organization with such powers, and to make this organization work efficiently.*

Such are the necessary corollaries of the four fundamental concepts laid down by Roosevelt and Churchill in the Atlantic Charter, which *ipso facto* were raised from the level of internal law to that of international law.

The principal object of international law is, therefore, to guarantee:

Freedom from fear (freedom from anxiety, right to peace and tranquillity);

Freedom from want (freedom from poverty, guarantee of comfort by satisfaction of minimum requirements for decency in human living);

Freedom of speech (freedom of thought and its expression by all means, abolition of instruments of repression);

Freedom of worship (freedom of belief and form of worship).

These four freedoms will constitute a Bill of Rights under international law.

Thus the object of international law is to establish security between nations on principles of justice, so that in each nation each individual may have peace, work, and liberty of thought and belief.

Having sketched the principles of international law, we will turn to the persons, goods, and juridical acts, and afterward to an organic framework that would make possible the functioning of such a system of law.

THE RULE

SINCE international morality should be the same as private morality, and international law consistent with the domestic law of each country, there is no reason why the same rules should not be established in international law as hold in domestic law. These are:

International law emanates from a deliberative body or International Assembly, is presumed to be universally known, and binds everybody who is in terms subject to it.

The nations, associations or groups of nations and international autarchies are responsible for the carrying out of the international principles in the territory under their jurisdiction.

When the date on which it becomes binding is not stated in the international law itself, it is understood to be so many days after the publication of the law by the office in the international official newspaper.

Any law is retroactive only if it expressly so provides and only to the extent that it does so provide.

International custom is characterized by understanding among civilized nations and has the strength of law in so far as it does not conflict with international law.

A general international principle is only compulsory when included in the laws or sanctioned by usage.

International juridical acts bind the parties to the proceeding.

THE PERSONS IN INTERNATIONAL LAW

WE WILL now deal with the persons who have to be considered in international law. They are the following:

(a) the international body politic (superstate);
(b) natural persons.*
(c) nations;
(d) groups or leagues of nations;
(e) international autarchies.

THE SUPERSTATE

The international body politic actually exists and is legally in formation. It had its subconscious origin in the conception of the needs for unified law. It came into view as the first Hague Convention, took shape in the League of Nations and is now being organized with powers of sanction. In other words, the superstate is now becoming the effective political power in the international sphere.

The whole tendency of mankind has been to widen out its circles—commercially, socially and politically—in the direction of world integration. Evolution in this connection from the tribe to the great nations is characteristic and indisputable, and it has long been possible to foresee the eventual "one world."

---

* "Persons" in law covers everyone to whom rights and obligations are attributed. As certain fundamental rights of the human being are recognized in the international sphere (Atlantic Charter), natural persons acquire personality under international law, as well as under private law.

There are various processes by which this point is reached, but they may be arranged in three groups: *(a)* conquest by a stronger nation; *(b)* confederation of nations; *(c)* superimposition of one power over national powers.

If this broadening out had been historically inevitable, there would have been no reason for opposing the nation which sought through the recent war to conquer the world, because we are going to reach, through the United Nations, the point that Hitler would have reached. And on that supposition the United Nations should be held responsible for opposing an inevitable evolution and thereby causing the shambles of 1939–45.

There are fundamental differences, however. Hitler started from the "master race" and from the supremacy of the state over the individual—oppression as a right of the state.

The United Nations reacted against the supremacy of the "master race" and against the oppression of the individual by the state. They started from the dignity of the human being as compared with any other human being, and as compared with the state—created to serve him and only having the right to use him within the limits of what is indispensable in order to serve him better.

Thus the starting points are diametrically opposite, and the similarity in the result, that "one world" is reached, is only apparent. In one instance we reach "one world" in which a single nation rules; the "master race" dominates the others, and denies human dignity, which can be destroyed by the domineering super-nation. In the other instance we arrive at "one world" guided by all the peoples, in which all races can live and which will serve all men.

The unification tendency has been tried out along all three channels—conquest, federation and the superimposition of a power which is consented to over national powers.

Conquest has always failed, whether by Caesar, Charlemagne,

Napoleon or Hitler. The impossibility of setting it up arises from its lack of a moral basis. Without a moral basis, moral forces must bring force against it and destroy it.

Federation also failed in the inconsequential attempts made. It has a moral basis, because it is by consent; but it can be undone by the withdrawal of that consent.

The superimposition of a power over national powers has been attempted. The Pope once exercised such power over the Christian world. It was found, however, that the unification of spiritual power with temporal power was dangerous, and intellectual evolution abolished that supremacy. The League of Nations was a more serious attempt. It failed, however, because it did not reach the point of laying its foundations on *man,* from whom it should have derived moral force. It lacked universality because it was only a League, to which adherence was voluntary and from which withdrawal was voluntary. It lacked effective strength to enforce its decisions. The very obligation to carry out its decisions was fundamentally illogical: the decisions of the League were binding *only upon its members, and only in the event of a unanimous vote,* so that only where compulsion was not needed, because all were in agreement, was a decision compulsory. If later a member that had taken part in a unanimous vote withdrew that assent, it had only to withdraw from the League, and the decision ceased to bind it after two years from the withdrawal. The decision remained binding on the other members, not because it was compulsory but because they fulfilled it voluntarily! (See Alberto Americano, in the São Paulo newspaper *Correio Paulistano,* under the title Post-War Legal Problems.)

As to the historical process, these forms have their origin in the tradition of power exercised by tacit consent; their place is taken by usurped power; by reaction they return to power under tacit consent, which finally should set up powers by express consent.

Nations, as an international community, have had over them authority given by tacit consent—the authority of the Pope over the Christian states in the Middle Ages; usurped authority—the conquests of Napoleon and of Hitler in Europe, forcing the authority of the conqueror upon them; and reasserted authority, which, in the case of the coalition against Napoleon, did not reach the point of being established internationally, having been dissolved after victory. In the case of the Allies against Germany in 1914–18, it approached the phase of authority by express consent with the formation of the League of Nations, but this proved too weak to sustain itself. In the present case, that of the United Nations, it will be tacitly based on the recognition of an international community, the structure of which will emerge from the San Francisco and subsequent conferences.

Like all persons, this international community has to have its place in time and space, that is, it has to have duration and to exert influence within a particular zone.

Its duration in time begins once various nations meet together, with a supernational outlook implying partial renunciation of sovereignty, and the new body emerges.

Although not yet possessing definite structure, the collective entity "United Nations" is already seen as a personality distinct from its components. Its will as a *de facto* entity is to a certain point independent of the national will of the members, for the collective body will be allowed to act in the common interest independently of the private interests of each people.

Its action in space is based outside the territory of any nation: on the ocean, which has always been recognized as well outside national domain, and in the air, which at the distance of the stratosphere is inaccessible to effective national sovereignty. Space is practically internationalized.

Thus the international community, with its nucleus in the United Nations, has:

(a) a tacit incipient will, existent in time as a body politic;

(b) an object—the effective realization of international law;

(c) effective action as a body, distinct from the action of each member nation;

(d) the high seas as an area of recognized jurisdiction—the ocean being a common domain, and freedom of the seas being essential to the international dominion—and the air as an area of jurisdiction which is beginning to be recognized.

The international order thus possesses all the characteristics of a juridical person.

We, therefore, conclude that the superstate is constituted by the community of nations, and possesses political power derived from consent through voluntary limitation of national sovereignties. This power will be exercised by three distinct agencies: the International Assembly, the Security Council and the Supreme Court.

THE INDIVIDUAL

The Atlantic Charter established that humanity must, for its own security, defend four basic principles: *freedom from fear, freedom from want, freedom of speech, freedom of worship.*

According to this proclamation, man should be free to express his thoughts and to exercise his religion. In order to enjoy this freedom he must be set free from fear; his mind must be set at rest as to whether peace will be maintained, and he must be sure of a means of livelihood. These are indispensable conditions for the free expression of thought and the free exercise of forms of worship.

Intellectually and juridically, these four principles do not actually constitute a novelty. For centuries man has been struggling for liberty of thought and religion; and such liberty already has a place, as a prerogative recognized by public law, in each national Constitution containing a Bill of Rights. Man has been struggling in the field of economics to establish juridical principles for guaranteeing freedom from want (social welfare law), and he has been struggling in international politics (arbitration treaties, political agreements, etc.) and on a wide literary front to bring about the establishment of peace in the world.

Yet it has been found that in spite of constant statements and much action, peace in the world has not yet been achieved; man is not free from want, nor is he everywhere assured freedom of thought or worship.

These conditions exist because the debates, economic measures, legislative precepts, and statements of the rights of man are not universally recognized.

Therefore the selfish indulgence by only one nation, or even by powerful private interests, in practices which disturb world economy is enough to spread poverty to the remotest parts of the world.

No sooner does a national Constitution declare the state to be an end in itself and man to be a means for serving that end, and at the same time deny to the individual the right to think differently from official thought or to exercise any religion varying from the official religion, than not only the nations themselves suffer, but processes of violence burst through frontiers and set up that universal tension which is the forerunner of war.

What is fundamentally new, therefore, about the Atlantic Charter, is not its statement of basic principles of human dignity; it is the transference of these principles to the international plane, for now they have been affirmed, not merely in the internal order of each country, but in the face of a world war, as basic elements for world peace.

Whereas until now international law had only considered relations between states with absolute sovereignty, the Atlantic Charter presents a new person in international law who had never before been considered—the human being. It presents him dignified by a statement of essential material and moral rights—the right to tranquillity, the right to a decent life, the right to think and the right to believe.

And just as no state must be allowed to organize itself to deny people these essential rights, so it becomes internationally established that the state is an instrument to serve the people and not an end for man to serve.

The outcome of this supreme conquest of the Atlantic Charter, therefore, is that the first person in international law, after the international superstate, is man, the natural person, and only after him comes the nation, which is committed to organizing itself into a state on foundations of respect toward human dignity, that is, on democratic principles. We do not hesitate, therefore, to place him first, immediately after the superstate in the order of persons in international law.

As to the four basic principles guaranteeing human dignity, their sole limit is that man is not free to destroy his own liberty. They cannot be renounced, because to renounce them would be to deny the object of international law.

THE NATION

It is extremely difficult to give a legal definition of what a nation is. There are typical nations, characterized by certain unmistakable elements such as territory, people, national consciousness consolidated chiefly by racial, historical, linguistic, religious and cultural unity, and sovereign government.

Not all the nations in the world, however, bear all these characteristics. Switzerland lacks racial and linguistic unity; the United States lacks religious unity, and up to a certain point racial and cultural unity, because of the immigratory influx. China lacks a united national consciousness. The Jews call themselves a nation, yet they have no national territory, and the "Jewish people" is made up of the most varied elements— German, Polish, Russian, Palestinian and other Jews.

Poland, until 1918, lacked sovereignty. The Czechoslovak nation was created artificially by the Treaty of Versailles, which gave it sovereignty and territory.

Three elements may be noted in the artificial formation of Czechoslovakia, however, which show the political idea—territory, people and sovereignty. One element is perhaps lacking— unified national consciousness—which transforms a population into a nation. It is the continuous existence of national consciousness which preserved Switzerland as a nation.

However, there are nations with no national consciousness, but which possess *territory, population and sovereignty,* and these elements constitute them as states. For legal-political purposes in the international structure, some such starting point is needed, seeing that no better basis is available. It is empirical, and the cases not coming under it should be examined in due course as individual problems. Nations may be emancipated by obtaining sovereignty, or a nation-state may be broken up to form several nations—as, for instance, would be the case if Switzerland wished to form three separate states. Or a nation-state may be dismembered and united to neighboring nations, or reconstituted after its territory has belonged to several nations, as in the case of Poland in 1918.

The pragmatic starting point is, therefore, the *status quo*— the existing nation-state.

Sovereignty

A nation organized as a state is thus sovereign. *Sovereignty* in the international sphere is *self-determination.*

When we come to consider nations without sovereignty, we observe that their personality is recognized in principle in international law, but they lack juridical capacity to exercise it. Only a nation-state has sovereignty—which, in the international sphere, is what capacity is in private law.

Non-sovereign nations may therefore be divided into unemancipated nations of various shades (colonies, protectorates, etc.) and nations under *capitis diminutio,* that is, under control as a measure of prevention, safety, reparation and re-education for international social life.

While the individual members of such non-sovereign nations have their position as persons in international law and should, therefore, be represented in the world community or superstate, these nations themselves cannot be represented.

A regimen for non-sovereign nations cannot be rigidly fixed beforehand. As far as unemancipated nations are concerned, they must be treated in keeping with the minimum requirements of human rights as laid down in the four principles of the Atlantic Charter. As to nations under *capitis diminutio,* treatment should follow the same principles, save for the right on the part of the international community to compel them to work to restore what they have destroyed during the war.

Such treatment cannot be considered slavery, even though it involves serious restrictions on liberty.

Limits to Sovereignty

Sovereignty is limited in the domestic sphere by the obligation to set up a democratic order. In the domestic sphere sovereignty is the legitimate power over territory and population which constitutes a state of a nation.

In the foreign sphere it has, up to the present, been considered the unlimited right of a nation to shape its own destiny, without any intervention by other nations. This is absolute self-determination, and has resulted in:

(*a*) absolute liberty of state organization, in spite of contrary will on the part of the people of the nation;

(b) power to judge its own cause in international disputes;

(c) power to carry out its decisions by force against other nations.

Such concepts, however, have proved harmful to national and international order. To national order, because they hinder effective manifestation of a nation's will with regard to its own destiny, once an individual or group seizes the reins of government without popular sanction; to international order, because they allow it to be overturned if a given nation is strong enough to bring this about.

The recent war provided painful proof that such risks are not fanciful. Action on the part of the restraining and Allied nations was directed toward driving sovereignty back into its proper sphere, say, *legitimate* power over its territory and population, constituting the nation a state.

Such power in regard to territory is legitimate by traditional occupation (the *uti possidetis* principle, which triumphed in Brazil's boundary disputes). It is *legitimate* in regard to populations so long as it respects their minimum safeties as proclaimed in the Atlantic Charter—their right to comfort, peace, thought and worship.

Self-Determination and the Fundamental Rights of the Individual

The principle of self-determination is to be interpreted in the light of the moment at which it was promulgated—that of a struggle between two cultures, one maintaining the state as the supreme reason, and the other maintaining human dignity as the

supreme reason for the state. So it is not states which determine
themselves, but nations which determine themselves into states
by the decision of their people.

Moreover, the principle is to be interpreted in light of the
declaration, also made in the Atlantic Charter, that the international community has, as its chief duty, to guarantee to man
certain fundamental rights.

It necessarily follows that peoples are not free to renounce
their own liberty in favor of a dictatorship.

A people which renounces freedom of opinion and of belief
encourages the advent of dictatorship, and the advent of dictatorship will find that people submissive and capable of endangering, through war, the fundamental rights of the rest of
mankind.

It is true that human beings, at times individually and at
times collectively, prefer slavery. But considered in relation to
each man who surrendered his own liberty, the matter is of the
highest practical, as well as theoretical, importance.

In the political order, liberty cannot include the right of self-
enslavement. The man who votes for his own enslavement either
votes under duress, or votes because of degradation; in either
case, human dignity is affronted.

It is not only human dignity, in the internal order of each
state, that is affected. Experience proves, from time immemorial,
that when liberty is surrendered, either voluntarily or through
the use of force, there must be created, by way of compensation, such myths as these: that only absolute power can insure
the realization of great projects for the public benefit; that a
nation becomes great in proportion to its military power; that
only the strong nations survive; that the strong nations must
expand territorially; that only the strong nations are respected;
that war is the means of proving strength; that the national
dignity demands war, and so forth. Such myths as these bring
misfortune to other nations.

The surrender, even voluntary, of the freedom of labor, or

of political freedom, is therefore harmful to the international community. This community ought to limit sovereignty in such a way as not to permit the suppression of these freedoms.

While such suppression exists under governments which are founded upon oppression, the democratic governments proceed otherwise. Originating with the people, and of temporary tenure, they must respect human dignity—of the majority as well as the minority—for they depend upon the people and must serve the people under pain of defeat at the polls. If erroneous doctrines arise they disappear with the temporary governments that created them.

Civilized nations set time limits to labor contracts so as to avoid the danger that a man will tie himself perpetually, through improvidence or hunger, to a job or wage which in his later years may no longer satisfy him. The Atlantic Charter, therefore, proclaims freedom from want or the right to comfort; and this is incompatible with perpetual labor contracts.

In keeping with this, the Charter also establishes the duties of the international community to assure the right to work.

Such fundamental guarantees are incompatible with inequalities of civil rights between nationals and foreigners and between men of different races and beliefs, with the identification of a party with the state, and with lack of guarantees for the representation of minorities.

Inequality of civil rights means fewer rights for some than others, according to nationality, race and belief. Lack of guarantees for the representation of minorities, or the identification of a party with the state, means less freedom of opinion or belief for some than for others.

Thus international experience shows that only democratic governments can be recognized as legitimate; that is, governments *elected by the people,* for a *limited period of time,* which *respect human dignity.*

Their *election by the people* assures national self-determination, which is fundamental in the Atlantic Charter. National self-determination, based on the will of the people, must not be confused with state self-determination, which may be based only on the will of the government.

National self-determination is limited by the restriction forbidding alienation of the right to freedom, which in international law includes the *duty of being free.* Self-determination can therefore only take place democratically.

The *limiting of their duration* assures that the nation is consulted periodically, to find out if the people's will remains the same as it was initially. Without this limitation there can be no certainty that the initial self-determination continues valid.

The *security of minorities* assures not only respect of human dignity but also permanent facility for enlightening the majority. The majority must not enslave the minority by identifying the government with a party.

Effective self-determination, by periodical election, with guarantees for minorities is therefore fundamental for world order, in contrast with a pseudo self-determination by a vote to renounce the right to a future vote, and without guarantees for minorities.

Even so, it only assures man's minimum freedoms if it preserves the *triple division of powers* enunciated by Montesquieu —legislative, executive and judicial.

Submission to International Decisions

In the judicial process of every country in the world there exists the institution of the thing judged, or the intangibility of final judgment.

An individual, *A,* sues another, *B.* The judge gives judgment in favor of *A*. *B* appeals to a court, say of three judges, two of whom give judgment in his favor and the other of whom is overridden. From the point of view of hierarchy *B* has won, but arithmetically it is a draw, two judges of the second instance being in favor of *B*, against one judge of the first instance and one of the second in favor of *A*. Qualitatively, it may be admitted that the latter pair is of more value than the former, and that the judgment may be unjust. So further recourse is usually allowed the losing litigant; but when the end is reached there is always the same qualitative doubt. Theoretically, this doubt exists even if the decision is unanimous in every case, for clever argumentation may have led all the judges into error. Thus the internal legal organization of each country establishes a system of appeals for the correction of error, but there is nothing to prove that, in principle, the correcting sentence is right and the corrected sentence was wrong.

Yet, when the end of the process is reached, general security requires that the loser should accept the result, even if in his judgment or in divine judgment it is unjust. All that could be done was done to achieve justice. The final decision is, in formal principle, the expression of true justice, even if in the judgment of the loser or by omniscient judgment true justice has not been done.

We have to accept this as a result of human frailty, once those functionally responsible for the dispensation of justice have said their last word after a minute examination of the case; for the party to the case is presumed less apt, through interest or passion, while the critics lack the opportunity that the judges have for close examination, and the Almighty does not reveal Himself to guide the courts.

Courts similar to those of common justice will exist in international justice, and their final decision must, therefore, have the same value—because the nation party to the case is sentimentally biased or otherwise interested—and the "God of armies" should not be allowed to intervene. Trial by ordeal is no longer in vogue.

The submission to the decisions of international justice is undoubtedly a limit to sovereignty.

The Duty of Cooperation

Nations holding strategic bases, factories, mines or mineral deposits exercise an international responsibility by reason of that very fact. They cannot enjoy such advantages to the detriment of the international community.

It would be illegal for the United States to close the Panama Canal to world traffic, for Britain, by closing Gibraltar, to compel European trade to go around Africa to reach Asia, or for Turkey to close the Bosporus and so prevent traffic between the Black Sea and the Mediterranean.

Similarly, it would be illegal for a nation holding certain minerals and factories to refuse to supply minerals of war material to another nation holding a strategic base of international value, for the good of the international community.

It would be illegal for a nation to prohibit the Red Cross to act in its territory, or to prohibit the UNNRA from obtaining the scientific or technical material or the provisions it needed to succor some population overtaken by misfortune or disease.

It would be illegal for a nation that produced food or goods of prime necessity to corner or destroy them under pretext of overproduction.

Today no war of conquest is limited; it is an act of aggression against the world, just as in the individual sphere crime is an offense under public law. There are no just aggressions and claims become legitimate only when they are sanctioned by the community.

Rights and the means of imposing them are inseparable. No

one is allowed to execute rights with his own hands. War is not only a direct risk to the one attacked, but a world risk, whatever its origin, locality and extent. The recent war started with the conquest of Abyssinia, or in Japan's attack on China.

The duty to collaborate in order to impede war is therefore another limitation to sovereignty.

The Abolition of Neutrality

As a result of the recent war it is now established that to provoke war is an international crime.

Ruy Barbosa said that there is no room for neutrality between the crime of war and international law, and this principle is on the way to universal acceptance.

A result of the tendency to adopt this principle universally was the United Nation's intimation to neutral nations that asylum for war criminals and those responsible for the war would not be tolerated.

Further, experience has shown the uselessness and indeed the harmfulness of neutrality.

In no case did neutrality prevent aggression against neutrals themselves. Each aggression brought about fresh reactions, until virtually the whole world entered the war. That is what will happen from now on; the involvement of all in war has been, is, and will be inevitable. Neutrality did not and will not prevent it; each neutral nation will be attacked successively and will enter the war successively. What happened this time leads to the conclusion that neutrality involves greater risks than immediate cooperation.

Aggression against one nation now means potential aggression against all others.

Even on the ground of utility and efficiency, it is better that all nations be involved simultaneously in a war, than one by one; and simultaneous entry means the abolition of neutrality.

In domestic law, where common securities are affected, neutrality is not possible—it does not exist; for the community intervenes either directly through a jury or by delegation through a criminal judge.

Taking as a starting point the view that aggression by one nation against another is in itself an international crime which concerns the international community, and the fact that this community can only be efficient through the support it receives from the component nations, we reach the conclusion that national neutrality in the presence of a war is an act of non-cooperation, constituting a crime of omission against the community. This reasoning from the international moral order, however, is not the only point against neutrality.

Through the tremendous speeding-up of the means of transport, distances have been so shortened that no nation is free from the risks of a war begun on the other side of the world. The nations are shut up in a tiny little world which is vulnerable at every point.

When in a small group in a closed room one man begins to fight another, simple prudence recommends flight or hiding behind a piece of furniture. If this is impractical, a cloak of indifference or preoccupation may be assumed as protection against being considered a partner in the fight. In the latter case, if there is a feeling of insecurity, it may be preferable to take sides. Against the weaker? Or against the aggressor? A sense of right demands the latter action.

Even so, there will be little chance of overcoming the aggressor unless there is a similar attitude on the part of the others present. Such a decision will be taken only if some link already exists among the men in the supposed group. It will not be taken by strangers, accidentally met together. It will be taken, say, by members of the same family, by workmen or students at leisure suddenly provoked or attacked.

Consider the same case in the international sphere. The first instinctive step—flight—is out of the question. A nation on the other side of the globe from the conflict is in the midst of it. Refuge cannot be taken on other planets. Shelter behind natural or artificial obstacles is not enough. Norway, away from the usual sphere of world conflict and protected by the sea, was attacked and conquered. The Maginot and Siegfried lines were flanked or crossed. The mountains of Switzerland would have been no obstacle to Germany if the route had happened to suit her; parachutists, artillery, aerial bombing and flying bombs have abundantly proved this. During the period of German aggression and that of Allied reaction, no obstacle, natural or artificial, was allowed to stand in the way. England escaped invasion only because Germany at the beginning of the war lacked the technique and the apparatus which the United Nations later perfected, and because they fortified themselves with such determination. The alternative of refuge behind bulwarks is, therefore, unsatisfactory, whether in the case of the individual in the illustration, whose refuge may easily be perforated by a bullet, or in the case of the nation, whose ramparts can be crossed by air and destroyed by land and air bombing. Armed neutrality is thus ineffective.

The third attitude—indifference to the dispute and unarmed neutrality—does not deserve discussion. It is enough to mention Denmark, Norway, Holland, Luxembourg and Belgium.

There remains the fourth attitude. It has its dangers, but it holds out more promises of success, if taken immediately by all the components of the group: individuals (in our illustration), and nations in the world sphere.

For all the components of a group to take it rapidly and in conjunction, it is necessary that a link exist—group consciousness. If they are unknown to one another they will not possess this attitude. If they have a common link, actual adjustment will be unnecessary; they will act together at the first attack, and will, therefore, win.

It was this group consciousness of the international community which was lacking at the beginning of the late war; it came into being during the war. The security of each and every nation is based on it.

The right to be neutral is contrary to international consciousness. The international community denies the existence of such a right.

It may be objected that this doctrine, though legitimate in principle, has been proved by experience to be dangerous; that, for instance, Switzerland's neutrality reduced her risk, while France's intervention in favor of Poland did not keep Poland from disappearing from the map, and caused France herself to disappear temporarily.

We disagree for the following reasons:

(1) In the last war each nation attacked defended itself alone, making it easy for the conquering aggressor of each to attack the others, one by one, whereas if there had been immediate joint action the result might have been different.

(2) The idea of neutrality still existed in international affairs and so the aggressor nation did not conceive of the prospect of a world coalition against her, with the intimidating effect that would have had.

(3) The world has not yet adopted all the security measures needed for effectively abolishing the neutrality idea.

(4) The aggressor nation's neighbors who were subjected to the greatest risk of attack also did not conceive of a prospect of a general coalition in their favor. They preferred the supposed lesser risk of declaring themselves neutral to an attitude of immediate reaction in sympathy with the attacked nation, with its possibility of similar reprisals. But it proved that a declaration of neutrality does not prevent the same fate. Denmark, Norway, Holland, Belgium and Luxembourg are examples. If we count the European nations that remained neutral —Sweden, Eire, Switzerland, Portugal, Turkey and Spain—we arrive statistically at a 50 per cent probability of not being

respected by the aggressor. It must be noticed, however, that the geographical situation modifies the statistical calculation. This is clear if we ask whether these probabilities would not have been reversed had the geographical situation been reversed. The answer is so self-evident that we are forced to the conclusion that it was not neutrality but geographical position which protected the neutral countries; and no one can say what nation will be the aggressor tomorrow, or which nations will be her neighbors.

(5) The neutrality tradition in international law ought to have been discarded, and its place taken by cooperation, when Italy invaded Abyssinia, Japan attacked China, or Germany seized Austria. Then there would not have been time for planning the coming aggressions, and the mood of aggression which produced the recent war would have been cut off at its source.

Summing up, we have, therefore, established the following:

Sovereignty, under international law, is political power of self-determination possessed by the nation-state for making laws, seeing that they are carried out, and vindicating them when violated, in regard to national territory and its inhabitants and visitors, within the limits formed by principles of international political order.

In the absence of state organization, sovereignty should be transferred to the superstate until a fresh state organization is formed.

It may be permanently withheld, when the fundamental requisites of independent national existence are lacking, or when a nation is put under police, security or restrictive action.

Essential Features of the National Organization

The following features must be assured by the international order:

(a) the threefold organization of legislative, executive and judicial power;

(b) the protection afforded by a Bill of Rights to a person in international law;

(c) the temporary character of elective functions;

(d) the derivation of executive and legislative power from the vote;

(e) non-identification of party and state;

(f) proportional representation of minorities;

(g) submission to the decisions of the International Court of Justice;

(h) submission to the laws of the International Assembly;

(i) duty to cooperate with the superstate.

These limits do not bar others which may become necessary to human dignity and international security.

The Birth and Death of Nations

The division of a nation into two or more nations as a voluntary pacific act must not depend on the superstate. To avoid the use of such a process as an artificial means of obtaining increased power in international affairs, the newly formed nations should be admitted immediately to the community only if the confirmation by the superstate is made by the Deliberative Assembly with a clause for immediate representation.

This confirmation would be based on an examination of the conditions—territory, people and sovereignty.

If the superstate would confirm the division but did not consent to immediate representation, it might fix a time for this—so many years as from the division. Representation would then begin automatically at the end of the period fixed, unless a two-thirds or other large majority of the Assembly extended the period. In the absence of confirmation, the right of representation would be acquired by the continuance of the new independence for a given number of years, unless a longer period up to twice that time were established by a large majority of the Assembly.

Division by violence would not be recognized unless carried out in legitimate self-defense in the case of large homogeneous ethnical or cultural groups subject to unequal civil or political treatment. In such a case, division might be approved by the superstate by a large majority decision.

If there is to be equality of treatment, such groups should only be allowed to appeal officially to the superstate for independence if they would fulfill the following conditions: *(a)* a decided majority localized in a given territory; *(b)* a common national consciousness; *(c)* a high educational standard with a high level of literacy.

Once the separation was effected, confirmation and representation would only be granted under the same conditions as in the case of peaceful voluntary separation. Until representation was effected for the separated nation, there should not be any representation except for the nation from which it broke off. For any alteration of such lines a large majority vote in the Assembly should be required.

In the absence of any other easily recognizable criterion, the nation retaining the capital city should be considered the original nation, and the other the separated nation. However, preference would be given to the terms of the agreement entered into by the separating nations as to which should preserve representation before the superstate during the interim period, unless otherwise determined by a large majority of the Deliberative Assembly.

Scattered ethnical, political or cultural minorities should not be granted the right to apply for separation.

The death of a state could occur only: *(a)* by voluntary annexation, after the requisites of voluntariness had been verified by the international community, or (*b*) by a decision of the international community under a large majority vote of the Assembly.

GROUPS OR ASSOCIATIONS OF NATIONS

Up to a certain point, fear of permitting the formation of groups or associations of nations is justified.

There are various kinds of interests which may draw nations together in groups: economic, military, racial, geographical or cultural.

Racial interests should be ruled out from the start. Race politics begin with the exaltation of race, result in the formation of race prejudices, and end in racial struggles.

Geographical interests are to a large extent interwoven with military, economic and cultural interests, and should be considered with these.

Military interests may be twofold—expansionist interests, which must be repressed, and cooperation for mutual defense, with certain geographical peculiarities taken into account. Such is the organization of the Pan American Union in this respect, because of the extent and vulnerable nature of the American coastline and the relative weakness of several American nations.

From the point of view of the international community the Pan American Union must be recognized as a valuable unit, because it is expressly devoted to the principle of settlements by arbitration, looks upon war exclusively as a system of mutual defense, and rules out any kind of aggressive effort.

The same conclusion will be reached regarding the cultural coordination promoted by the Pan American Union, which has in view the dignifying of man.

When considering economic interests we must be careful to distinguish the cases in which a group or association of nations conceals the formation of international trusts or cartels from those in which coordination and guidance of mutual economy is affected in such a way as to benefit the international community.

Especially so far as the Pan American Union is concerned it should be noted that its policy has been such as to serve as a model for the international community.

We have thus shown that the organization of regional or continental groups or associations is beneficial, provided they favor the international community, keeping in line with its basic principles and being subject to review by it as to points which may endanger it.

The chief feature which should distinguish this type of juridical person in international law is its non-possession of sovereignty. This remains in the hands of the component nations.

INTERNATIONAL AUTARCHIES

Autarchy is an autonomized public service. The international community will exercise a number of functions, and among these some will be best carried on by an entity which is an autarchy.

An example of this is UNRRA. UNRRA is an international entity resulting from an agreement among forty-four nations to facilitate the organization of the resources of the United Nations in such a way that the liberated nations may have equal opportunities to mitigate the sufferings of their population and prepare their reconstitution in peace.

It is authorized by the member nations to operate during the period of the war under solicitation from the military authorities, and, after the war is over, under solicitation from, or agreement with, the authorities of the liberated nations.

The agreement reads :

"Agreement for United Nations Relief and Rehabilitation Administration.

"The government or authorities whose duly authorized representatives have subscribed hereto,

"Being United Nations or being associated with the United Nations in this war,

"Being determined that immediately upon the liberation of any area by the armed forces of the United Nations, or as a consequence of retreat of the enemy the population thereof shall receive aid and relief from their sufferings, food, clothing and shelter, aid in the prevention of pestilence and in the recovery of the health of the people, and that preparations and arrangements shall be made for the return of prisoners and exiles to their homes and for assistance in the resumption of urgent needed agricultural and industrial production and the restoration of essential services,

"Have agreed as follows:

"There is hereby established the United Nations Relief and Rehabilitation Administration."

The agreement is dated November 9, 1943, and signed by forty-four governments.

This instance is sufficient to justify the creating of a new entity under international law—the *international autarchy*.

PROPERTY

INTERNATIONAL PROPERTY *

LIKE NATIONS, the superstate possesses territory in the broad sense—sea and air—and should possess territories not yet appropriated.

* This chapter is partly based on a conversation with Salvador Mendieta, President of the University of Nicaragua.

International property therefore includes:

(1) *The oceans.*

The oceans have always been considered common property in international order. The *freedom of the seas* has been secured by common consent or by international treaties and conventions. This was seen in the repression of piracy. The seas have always been considered free.

(2) *Straits and canals of international value.*

The freedom of the seas implies the freedom of straits and of artificial canals having access to the sea.

Although Britain has had virtual control of Gibraltar, Suez and Singapore since the last century, and the United States similar control of the Panama Canal Zone this century, freedom of passage for world trade has been assured. The same situation must hold for the Bosporus, Russia's outlet from the Black Sea to the Mediterranean, the Skagerrak, the Kattegat and the Sound giving access to the Baltic, and the Strait of Magellan at the southernmost end of South America.

Germany, fearing the closing of her outlets, built the Kiel Canal, which is obviously an international base.

The *de facto* and *de jure* situation is, therefore, freedom of passage through straits and canals of international value.

(3) *The air.*

For the formation of air law in international order, analogies have been sought between territorial waters and territorial air.

The question of territorial air space is not of great importance from the point of view of national sovereignty, seeing that once the population's interests are protected the air space at high level should belong to the community, and at low levels should be placed at the disposal of the community when necessary. It is important, however, from the point of view of risk in the case of aggression, and from that of repressive action by the community against an aggressor.

Provided, therefore, that the nation's population and wealth are given security, air space is international; and just as no nation has possessed the right to hinder ocean navigation, whether military or not, beyond its own territorial waters, so no nation should have the right to hinder air navigation, whether it be commercial navigation or military control by the international community, in the upper air space at a height safe for population and property.

This is the conclusion to be arrived at from the analogy of the already existing right of freedom of the seas, and from the new concept of the inadmissibility of neutrality.

(4) *Land not yet appropriated by a nation.*

It is very unlikely that such land exists, but it must be mentioned.

(5) *Land and buildings* of the international community necessary for its activities.

(6) *Property* belonging to it under the regime of common right.

PROPERTY OF INTERNATIONAL VALUE OR UNDER INTERNATIONAL CONTROL

There are also properties of international value which are to be supervised by the international community as follows: These are

(1) *Military bases* for guaranteeing liberty of oceans, straits and canals.

Ocean space would not secure effective liberty of the seas or continuity of existence of the authority claimed against usurpation, unless it had certain bases on land and certain strategic points. Such have been in the hands of Britain, but at the service of the international community: the two entrances to the

Mediterranean Sea (Suez and Gibraltar) and the intermediate point, Malta, assuring free route from Atlantic Europe to Indian Asia; and Singapore, which guarantees navigation between the Pacific and Indian oceans; Panama, in the hands of the United States, permitting Pacific-Atlantic communications; the Strait of Magellan, for Pacific-Atlantic communications to the south of the Americas. With the acceleration of means of transport and increased risk of attack against the freedom of the seas of the international community, other points have become vital, such as Natal (Brazil) and Dakar where the Atlantic narrows between South America and Africa.

If Germany had been able to seize Suez, as she intended to do through Rommel's attack on Egypt; Gibraltar, as she planned to do when she favored the accession of Franco as dictator of Spain; Dakar, which she succeeded in maintaining at her service for a long time in the hands of the Vichy Government; the Strait of Magellan, through Axis policy in the Argentine; and Panama, which her ally Japan had in view and which was full of Japanese fishermen—if Germany had succeeded in getting these vital points, she would have cut off all possibility of free navigation in the world, for Singapore was already in her hands, having been seized by Japan soon after the latter's entry in the war.

As she was unsuccessful in this she was unable to consummate her usurpation of international authority over the seas. Her failure secured the possibility of the formation of an international authority as desired by the components of the United Nations.

Similarly, domination of the air by the international community demands a foothold on land, at some of the ocean bases already mentioned, which are equally vital for the control of the air. In addition, a few more points in mid-ocean would be necessary, such as Iceland for the North Atlantic, the Azores for the mid-Atlantic, perhaps St. Helena for the South; Honolulu for the North Pacific, the Marquesas or Tuamotu for the Central Pacific, and some base in New Zealand for the South; and bases on Madagascar and Kerguelen for the Indian Ocean.

The preservation of the freedom of straits and canals has been assured by the construction of military bases adjoining them, as in the case of Gibraltar, Singapore and Panama, and the principle of free navigation has always been followed in peacetime. The oceans will not be free if the freedom of the straits is not assured, and the latter are therefore essentially international.

The maintenance of their international status, *de facto* and *de jure, depends, however, on the principle that the adjoining military bases are also of international interest and must, therefore, serve the latter.* Hence the need for the nations that hold such regions or geographical units to consider themselves as trustees of international rights and interests, in the service of the international community. It is worth noting that in the recent war Brazil gave tacit assent to this principle when she recognized the need for the control of the Atlantic in view of the risk of attacks by the country that was violating international law and granted the restraining nations the use of the Natal base, opposite the Dakar base, then under German-Vichy control.

A case such as this must, therefore, be considered from the point of view of the new concept of *national property with an international value.*

The idea of territorial waters begins to lose interest from the point of view of sovereignty, in view of the new concept of the international community, and of the condemnation of neutrality as incompatible with it. Any nation should be prepared to cede its land and territorial waters to the community, not only in defense of the latter but also in self-defense.

(2) *Rivers, inland seas and lakes* giving access to inland countries.

(3) *Rail and other roads and airfields* giving access to inland countries.

(4) *Strategic industries, mines and deposits* of international value.

The second and third cases just mentioned above call for no special justification, as they follow from what has been set out already.

The existence of certain types of wealth in the subsoil creates a most valuable military privilege for certain nations, and a potential danger for the international community.

Mines of strategic minerals are, therefore, by their very definition property of international value. They are, however, always situated in national territory, and this calls for the establishment of a delicate but efficient system of control, in the interests of world security.

The first step toward such security is to nationalize mining and other industries which can in any way be used for war.

This, however, is not sufficient. Private concerns interested in creating markets for their products by means of war might be supplanted by direct ownership of the state, which could manufacture arms for its own benefit, to sell to others or to make war on its own account, and the evil would continue.

As they are of interest to international order, war industries, mines and deposits constitute property of international value just as international military bases do. Although each nation holds and exploits them, it can only be permitted so long as it does not jeopardize international order. This is the reason for making legitimate the internationalization and actual international occupation of such properties in such cases, the dismantling or removal of the factories, interdiction of mines and deposits, or their exploitation by the international entity, either directly or through agents.

PROTECTION OF NATIONAL AND INDIVIDUAL PROPERTY

In view of the system proposed for international law it is also necessary that the minimum securities for national and individual property be defined.

They may be stated as follows:

National property. International law should secure to the nations the enjoyment of their national property and riches, protecting them against usurpation.

Individual property. Nations should, under international supervision, secure to all men the possibility of enjoying the material and non-material property and riches which are indispensable to the maintenance and dignity of life.

JURIDICAL FACTS

IN INTERNATIONAL order juridical facts are all occurrences capable of originating, terminating or altering a juridical relation, or of producing a juridical effect of an international nature.

Juridical facts are of two kinds:

(1) Juridical acts per se;

(2) Facts independent of juridical acts.

A juridical act is an act done by a capable agent, in juridical form, which has as its scope a lawful object in international order.

Acts which violate the principles of international public order, and those which are brought about through coercion, are null and void.

A juridical act can be undone under the same conditions as those required for its doing. When it is initially bilateral, or becomes so through the adherence of a second party, agreement between the parties is needed for its rescission.

When modification of conditions existing at the time of the act calls for alteration or rescission, this may be carried out under rescission by the International Court apart from considerations of bilaterality or of agreement.

A fact independent of juridical act may be natural or produced. A produced act may be *licit* or *illicit,* and the latter may be a restricted *illicit act* or an act *harmful to the community.*

Restricted illicit acts are violations of law which do not constitute *harmful acts.* They may be of commission or omission.

HARMFUL ACTS

The concept of *harmful* acts cannot be precisely the same in international law as the definition of crime in each nation's domestic law.

The rule that there is no crime without a prior law defining it, and the rule that there is no penalty without prior legal commination, are not applicable to international law.

Such principles cannot hold, because the basis of the category *crime* is different from that of the category *harmful act* in international law, and because only in the individual sphere is there any restriction on the tools with which crime is perpetrated and on the possibilities of violating the rights of others.

In international law the possibilities become greater and greater as technical processes are perfected. Apart from specific agreement as to the fundamental rights of man, which international law sets out to secure, the permanence of the international community depends on such variable standards that the corresponding acts of violation cannot be predetermined.

Thus, when a possibility of danger arises, the international community must take steps to prevent it, and take the necessary action, even though this may not constitute a penalty in the strict sense of the word.

To avoid the objection that the responsibility of the perpetrator (individual or nation) of the harmful act should be defined by prior specification of the harmful act which is prohibited, the international community should employ *warnings,* which, once made, take the place of a prior law expressly defining all harmful acts.

As to previous prescription of penalties, this seems impossible under international law.

In domestic law the perpetrator should have previous knowledge of the harmfulness of the act and of its penal consequences, so that he can calculate the punishment and repress his criminal impulse.

In international law, if previous knowledge is to be achieved by means of a warning, the violator will receive *ipso facto* notice of the maximum consequences—intervention—to whatever extent may be necessary.

Further, an act committed by a weak nation may call for less energetic or extensive repressive action than the same act when committed by a strong nation.

A nation is by definition a responsible body to the fullest extent of the term, and in principle is capable of foreseeing the maximum consequences and of deciding to bear them. A nation should always anticipate maximum repressive action and be intimidated thereby.

Lastly, it is not the idea of punishment which is in view, but that of security—international security assured by police measures of security, repressive action and restoration. Such measures as may be appropriate for the purpose in view are, therefore, applicable.

The following list of *acts harmful to the community* is not exhaustive:

Violation of the principles contained in the Declaration of the Rights of Man (four principles of the Atlantic Charter);

Propaganda destructive of those principles;

Inequality of civil rights for nationals and foreigners or between races or classes;

Threats to international public health;

Slavery;

White-slave traffic;

Provocation of disquiet, disorder or terror; provocation or aggravation of national sentiments in an aggressive manner;

Commission of brutal acts, violation, plunder, arson or shooting, with disturbing effects on international order;

Formation of parties or associations to disturb international political or economic order;

Economic restrictions calculated to disturb international economy;

Attempts against the independence or self-determination of a nation's government;

"Armamentism" either open or disguised as industrialism;

The elimination of democracy;

Identification of the dominant party with the state;

Colonial expansion;

Armed attack by one nation on another, even to exact an undoubted right;

Neutrality in the face of armed attack;

Arrangements as to war or rules of war;

Non-observance of decisions of any of the authorities of the international community, or refusal of collaboration toward the fulfillment of international law or maintenance of order;

Conquest, even by pacific means;

Protection of criminals of concern to the international community;

Tolerance of the harmful acts referred to above within its territory;

Refusal of passage for international forces and their necessary adjuncts through its territory.

This list is too self-evident to require any explanations, but we will consider certain special cases.

WAR

DECLARATION AND REGULATION

So LONG as it is admitted that war constitutes a harmful act, there is no need to consider whether it was preceded by a declaration of war on the part of the aggressor or not.

It is, however, the duty of the nation attacked to inform the international community simultaneously with the first act of defense, in order to obtain sanction for its acts, which will thus become delegated acts.

As to regulations for war, it must be understood that to regulate war as war would be the same as for the Penal Code to regulate dueling.

There is thus established the non-juridical character of the principle that acts of war are legitimate *for both sides* provided they respect certain technical rules and principles of humaneness. There is no such thing as *ethics of crime,* and so *ethics of war* cannot exist in law.

Besides the crime of making war, there may occur within the war criminal acts of cruelty or inhumanity serving as an indication of the need for intensifying the measures of repression and security. These should involve direct punishment of the responsible persons, as international crimes occurring concurrently with the crime of war.

Regulations for war, therefore, are limited to regulations of *police powers.* This concerns the international community, whose duty is to demand respect for the fundamental principles of international law. The limits of these police powers are thus those fundamental principles in so far as the *state of need* of the community and the exercise of the police powers (that is, the need for war operations) must include them.

PEACE TREATIES

So long as war was considered an "international relation" instead of an *international harmful act,* treaties of peace were theoretically admissible. Two nations would *declare war,* that is, cut themselves off from normal relations and enter into a different kind of relation, equally regulated by the *laws of war,* which then came into force. Afterward they should contract to return to normal relations by a *peace treaty* laying down the bases of this return. It is a system which satisfies merely formal juridical concepts. All the rules were obeyed. "Vous avez raison, je n'ai pas tort, nous sommes d'accord"—except that the defeated signed the treaty because it had been defeated, that is, under coercion. Therefore, substantial juridical concepts are not satisfied in this way, for, according to them, coerced will prejudices the juridical act—the peace treaty in this case.

Each peace treaty is by its very existence the germ of a new war. The defeated nation breaks it and goes to war in order to reacquire its free will, which was coerced by the treaty, and so to restore the juridical order violated by the coercion it suffered. The winner, seeing the treaty broken, goes to war to restore the juridical order broken by the breaking of the treaty.

And so it goes on—a fresh declaration of war, fresh application of the laws of war, a fresh peace treaty, fresh coercion, fresh breaking of the treaty. "Si cette chanson vous embête . . ."

Having shown the non-juridical nature and the insecurity of treaties of peace under the old concepts of international life, let us consider them under the present concept of *harmful international acts* and their restraint up to the final restoration of peace and reparation of damage.

When a nation commits violation of rights which does not constitute an *internationally harmful act,* the injured nation either appeals to the international courts, or comes to an arrangement with the injuring nation as to the means of reparation, or waives reparation. A treaty thus made is lawful because it is not made under coercion, nor is the security of the community affected.

But when a nation commits an internationally harmful act, international security is in question. Neither the violating nation, the injured nation, nor the international community can make a *treaty covering crime or its repression.*

A *treaty covering crime* would have an illicit object; no legal system allows it.

A *treaty covering repression* would be something similar to intervention before the authorities on the part of the criminal, to regulate the penalty imposed on him.

It must not be thought that this is a mere question of form, and that what is actually done under the guise of a treaty is the application of the principles of repression, that is, of the penalty.

Let us first consider *surrender.*

It is inconceivable that a criminal, in the act of holding up his hands in surrender, should demand conditions without which he would not hand himself over. Conditions of surrender will be imposed in a similar way to that followed by authorities when overcoming and disarming a criminal.

Surrender, which is necessarily *unconditional,* will contain clauses—orders to be carried out—as in the case of the individual, who has to hold up his hands, give up his arms, allow himself to be searched for other arms, hold out his hands for handcuffs, and so on.

Surrender clauses are not binding in respect of principles of repression.

We will now consider the peace treaty from the point of view suggested, of the previous fixing of the principles of repression.

It has already been shown that in international law the system of establishing restraining principles *in genere* is impracticable because during war it is impossible to foresee the extent of use of weapons of attack, so that it cannot be decided *a priori* what is to be used to check them. They are military questions to be decided in the operations of war. It has also been shown that it is impossible to foresee all the measures for restoration; they depend on the contingencies of each case, in accordance with its extent and with changes required by changing times.

In the same way a peace treaty, as such, would be a reprehensible "leveling out" where the future cannot be foreseen, and would have the harmful psychological effect on world opinion of appearing, in the event of subsequent alteration, to constitute a violation of the word of the authorized organ of the international community.

Consequently, any decision imposed either at the time of surrender or, later, in the way of repression or reparation implies no agreement that it will not be modified or tightened up, and a clause ought to be included making this explicit.

LEGITIMATE DEFENSE

WARFARE AS LEGITIMATE DEFENSE

UNDER international law legitimate defense will be a reaction, expressly or tacitly authorized, in the name of international law, in anticipation of action by the community. It assumes present aggression and the absence of the effective power of the international police.

As a result of the growing universal conscience of moral obligations, nations that desire to perpetuate acts of aggression have attempted to convert world opinion in their favor by insinuating previous acts of aggression by their victims, to put themselves in a presumptive position of legitimate defense.

It is, therefore, necessary to consider with care what aggression is under international law.

In this sphere it is not possible to make defense legitimate by alleging *moral aggression*. Experience has shown that whenever there is intentional talk of moral aggression, offense, etc., actions of violence and injustice are behind it. In this case, as soon as international relations are broken, there should be a pronouncement by the International Court imposing the appropriate sanction.

Similarly, imminence of aggression, which according to the general modern idea makes self-defense legitimate, cannot do so in international law. In this case as well, experience has shown that supposed imminence of aggression may serve as a pretext for a war of aggression.

The arming of a nation can constitute an international peril, so that when a nation overarms itself the matter is of concern to the community before it concerns a neighboring country. It should be brought to the notice of the community, and it is the latter that will take the necessary steps, among which will be that of authorizing the threatened nation to increase its armaments, and delegating it authority to act until the community can come to its aid. The act of legitimate defense, in this case of imminence of aggression, should be *preceded* by express authorization.

Open or secret mobilization of military forces on the part of the victim has been another pretext for "legitimate" defense on the part of aggressor nations who are thus assumed to have merely stepped in before an imminent attack so that the reaction may be efficient.

Secret mobilization, however, should be brought to the notice of the community, in order to obtain authorization for legitimate defense, for it is not a visible act, and what must clearly distinguish legitimate defense is the evidence of the attack. If the imminence of the attack is not clear, there is no evidence; it is a matter for investigation by the community.

Open mobilization should, however, make open preparation on the part of the threatened nation permissible—that is, counter-mobilization—provided the threatened nation does not precipitate the attack. If it desires to forestall the attack it should obtain authorization and so acquire *police powers* until the community can act.

ACTUAL AGGRESSION

Actual aggression is aggression *against a nation's territory,* over land, sea and air, including blockade. Aggression *against a nation's subjects or interests outside its territory* is only imminent aggression. It may be merely captious. It may be provoked by the interested party itself. It may be a result of internal disputes or strife. It may be a mere question of domestic personal rights. The experience of the alleged oppression of German subjects in Poland is painfully significant as to the care needed in accepting accusations of this kind to justify any "defense." Such cases are for the community to judge, not for the supposed victim.

Actual aggression against a nation's territory makes acts of immediate reaction legitimate, whether in the territory of the attacked or of the attacking nation. Simultaneously, the victim nation must advise the community, and all the former's actions will continue to be considered legitimate until the community makes its definite pronouncement and provides effective assistance. After that pronouncement the attacked nation's acts will only be legitimate to the extent of the authorization given by the international community.

THE INJUSTICE OF AGGRESSION

In principle aggression involves injustice. Once a nation's territory is touched or blockaded, the aggression is presumed to be unjust and acts of repulsion to be legitimate. It is understood that there is tacit authorization for repulsion. The question of injustice, however, remains suspended until the international community makes its pronouncement. When the tacit authorization is ratified, the repulse is just; when it is refused, the supposed repulsion is considered to involve actual aggression.

In no case, therefore, is there any right of legitimate defense against a nation which acts by authority of the international community, or against direct action by the community.

In order to distinguish legitimate defense, the initial act of violence is a matter to be ascertained immediately. Anyone who sees another pull out a revolver reaches, without any difficulty, the conclusion that a risk exists. The only intelligent procedure is to check the use of the revolver. For the moment it does not matter whether the aggressor has right on his side or not. This is the same principle as that which, under principles of social stability, allows the use of injunctions against violators of property, even when the violator has a legal title to the property against the illegal holder. The law repels the assault on the property, even when it is the owner who assaults the peaceful holder. In order to act against the aggressor and prevent the possibility of aggression, it is not necessary to know if the aggression is made for a legitimate reason. It is the aggression itself which is absolutely illegitimate.

Similarly, if we were to see a man put his hand in another's pocket, and take something out of it, we would not refrain from turning him over to the authorities, even if we are told that what he has taken belongs to him. If the victim calls for help, the bystanders intervene without even inquiring why the aggressor put his hand in the victim's pocket. It is a question of justice, and only indirectly has justice to do with public order. Violence must not be practiced, even to exercise a right; instead of attacking, the party must seek without violence to obtain judicial means for the recognition of his rights. If he does not succeed, even if in principle justice and right are on his side, the final legal decision puts him definitely in the position of having no right; he cannot perpetrate aggression in order to do justice himself, on the ground that justice has been denied to him.

This fundamental principle of security, therefore, disassociates might and right; it imposes a pragmatic solution of conformity, as opposed to the ideal solution of justice.

As soon as the initial act of aggression takes place, all the nations of the world, being potential victims, whether near or far, should join together automatically as a single whole in the common cause, even without considering the principle of international solidarity, simply because of the likelihood of their all being affected one after another.

STATE OF NEED

Nations that have precipitated wars of aggression have usually created suitable myths and led their people to believe that they are in a state of legitimate defense. Such legitimacy, however, is not marked by its classical features in penal law.

Against the adversaries they attack, they allege the growing potentiality of the threat and that if they await the actual attack it will be impossible for them to defend themselves effectively, because their enemies will develop their power to the maximum and will only attack when they are sure defense is impossible.

Such arguments are always advanced when it is necessary to justify the fact of the "victim" having attacked before the "potential aggressor."

The fundamental defect of such arguments is that only the supposed victim believes in them. Everyone else ascertains a fact—the fact of aggression—and a fancy—that the attacked nation was preparing to attack.

The possibility should, however, be admitted in principle. In the international organization it will be considered, and such premeditated aggression prevented.

The international organization will need, by acts for general security, to hinder any nation from preparing by means of totalitarianism, and so becoming a constant threat to collective security.

If a threat from another nation is alleged, the measure should be applied to the nation, also if the allegation proves true. If a nation refuses, it must be compelled by intervention, as a restraining measure, and by occupation, as a security and re-education measure.

The following conclusions are, therefore, inevitable:

International law only recognizes a state of need in the case of legitimate defense.

Defense is legitimate for repelling actual attack on national territory over land, sea and air, including blockade, and should be immediately communicated to the international community. Defense remains legitimate until the community makes its pronouncement, and so soon as the community comes into action the attacked nation should act in concert with it.

Action against another nation to avoid worse consequences is illegitimate unless it has the nature of legitimate defense or, lacking this, is authorized by the international community.

LEGITIMATE DEFENSE OF PEOPLES BY REVOLUTION

History presents examples of whole populations or classes being subjected to oppressive regimes, and of so-called ethnical minorities situated in particular parts of the territory to whom have been denied civil and political rights on an equal basis with the population of the rest of the country.

Again, there have been instances of a nation provoking an international incident under the pretext that its subjects, located in another country, are under an oppressive regime.

It is essential that the international power should legislate upon these cases, as much for liberating oppressed populations as for preventing the creation of incidents under false pretexts.

Until recently such false pretexts made war between the provoking nation and the provoked legitimate, with other nations maintaining their neutrality.

When legitimate complaints of oppression led populations to revolt, they were considered matters of sovereignty, so that it was no other nation's business to intervene with a view to stopping the oppression. When finally the revolution gained sufficient power to dominate a considerable territory, the other nations considered the *de facto* situation as that of two nations at war, and took the position of neutrals.

The evil was and is clear in the case of a revolution resulting from oppression, from disrespect of the basic principles of human dignity. Since this dignity has not been guaranteed in the past, with the Atlantic Charter, which proposes to guarantee it, the case becomes one of violation of international law. It is, therefore, essential for international law to settle the following points:

In principle, revolution is contrary to international law because it is a process of violence.

A nation in which revolution breaks out may appeal to the community for aid in quelling it. If the community ascertains that there is democratic organization in the country concerned, and actual respect for the rights mentioned in the Bill of Rights (the four principles of the Atlantic Charter), it will give this assistance by means of its own intervention or by authorizing other nations to provide the needed aid.

Populations which revolt to restore the principles of the Bill of Rights, equality of civil and political rights and democratic practices, however, are considered to be acting in legitimate self-defense.

No help, whether open or disguised, can be given by other nations to a revolution until the legitimacy of the latter is recognized or intervention is declared by the community in favor of the revolution, and, even then, only with the authorization of the international community. In this case other nations will give their help in concert with the community.

PREVENTION, REPRESSION AND REPARATION OF EFFECTS OF HARMFUL ACTS—SECURITY MEASURES

IT IS for the state, under whose jurisdiction the agent functions, to prevent and restrain *harmful acts*. If there is negligence, deficiency or ineffectiveness in such prevention or restraint, it will be exercised by the international community.

It is for the international community to take security measures, and prevent, repress or make reparation for the effects of a harmful act done by a state, by associations or groups of states, or by the international autarchies, and also to decide what the security measures are to be. In special cases they may be delegation of authority by the community to one or more states.

All such measures are effected by means of *intervention*.

INTERVENTION

Intervention by the community against a violating nation is, in the first place, an *international police measure*. It has no limits other than those laid down by universal conscience, and is made legitimate by the extent to which it is actually effective.

It is necessary to distinguish between international action in *preventive measures, repressive measures, reparative measures* and *security measures,* which are imposed by the deliberative organ or called for by the judicial organ. At any rate at the present stage of international law there is no place for specific examples or previous legal specification.

Measures may range from warnings, pacific economic sanctions and breaking off of relations, to territorial intervention, occupation of factories, mines, deposits and territory, blockading and war. The limits are a matter of expediency and efficiency, within the precepts of humanity.

Measures of reintegration or security, corresponding to penalties under domestic penal law, consist of indefinite occupation, re-educative processes applied to the population, the imposition upon the latter of reconstruction labor in devastated regions, individual or collective transportation, and direct domination or domination under mandate (*capitis diminutio*).

Legal predetermination is not necessary, not only because if international law is considered to be known (a *juris et de jure* assumption) the consequences can be foreseen by the violator, but also because, at least for the present, it is impossible to determine a penalty beforehand to an internationally harmful act.

For this very reason, the possibility of revision must always be maintained, whether for strengthening, softening or eliminating such measures.

We shall, therefore, deal only with war as a repressive process, with reparations, and with the maximum effect either can produce—loss of political independence.

WAR AS A PROCESS OF REPRESSION

War has been regarded as a legitimate process for enriching a nation, by pillage and conquest of territories, as a means of imposing beliefs or political convictions, or of settling international disputes, and as a noble end in itself.

In the first instance it is equivalent to robbery, in the second to a violation of human dignity, in the third it implies the conviction that might is right, and in the last the conviction that might in itself constitutes the ideal of justice. In each of these cases war becomes a legal form of crime against mankind.

At the beginning of this century some internationalists outlined the concept that war is a crime of lese humanity, that to react is an act of legitimate defense and that to inhibit war is an international duty.

But as a matter of fact until now war has been considered a bilateral international act, an international relation by a process of violence on both sides.

The reformation of this concept presents war from two points of view: on the one hand, as an international act which is harmful and should be repressed, and, on the other, as an act of reaction as legitimate defense while the victim awaits help and acts in isolation, and of repression as soon as the community takes charge of the reaction.

In short, it is crime for one side and law for the other, legitimate defense being recognized as a power of the international police.

REPARATIONS

A nation which in spite of all preventive measures provokes war suffers the reaction of the offended nation as a measure of legitimate defense and that of the community as a measure of repression.

When the war is over, this nation may be subjected to measures of control, if sufficient, or to occupation as a measure of maximum security. These measures involve others, such as reparations of various kinds, of which the commonest are indemnities or reparation in kind, and re-education.

Indemnities may be imposed for direct payment by the nation-state itself, proportionately to the autonomy left to it, or may be collected by the administration which the community imposes. In the latter case we shall have, in international law, a juridical process similar to distraint in ordinary law.

Reparations in kind may also be imposed in both ways—by compelling the state which has done the damage to repair it, or by the international community undertaking the direction of the reparations.

The case may, therefore, arise of reparations requiring the requisitioning of workmen or experts from the defeated nation to carry out reparation work in the territory of the devastated nations.

The problem deserves attention because objections have been raised to it, the most important one being that—it is alleged—the measures are tantamount to the enslaving of the populations, classes or groups that are set to work and in any case to the humiliation of human personality.

It would not seem, however, that this is a parallel, apart from the historic fact of slavery having existed. It is an artificial rather than a real similarity.

Slavery transformed human beings into the property of other beings, who undertook to provide them with a minimum of clothing, food and shelter to preserve them in a fit state for producing work.

In the case in question there is no property vested in the winners; there is compulsion for the defeated to work for the community to which they really belong. As part of this community they do the work for remuneration, and are only denied a choice of work. It is the contribution demanded of the violating nation and falling on its inhabitants somewhat in the same way as compulsory military service.

Allegations of slavery have never been made against military service which, even though compulsory, is based on the solidarity between nation and citizen.

The same relation exists, for civil reparation service, between the citizen and the nation that did the damage: the nation that does damage by means of its citizens should make reparation for that damage by means of its citizens.

The fact of damage demands reparations, and the citizens make reparation for what they damaged. There was an identification of will between the nation and its citizens to cause the damage, and there remains as a consequence the same identification as to the responsibility to repair it.

It is clear that in this case reparation, being imposed, follows a government plan with all its drawbacks. Economic planning by government is a dangerous system in the normal life of a nation. When a nation is at war in self-defense it is considered a necessary evil.

It forms part of general mobilization. Engineers, chemists, mechanics, farmers, foremen and workmen are no longer free to choose the work they like best. They do the work that is considered most necessary for the winning of victory; yet they are not responsible for the war.

In the case of reparations and so-called forced labor on the part of the defeated, there will simply be the mobilization of the defeated for repairing the damage done. In this damage there is collective responsibility on the part of each citizen, as we have already pointed out.

Therefore, there is no cause for alarm in the measure of mobilization needed for reparations. It did not operate when the youth of the nation that was attacked, who were not responsible for it, were forced to go to war, whence they would return mutilated, or would never return.

And so it is contrary to international morality that such a question should arise about reparations and the need for mobilizing the nation that is responsible. The new conception would make it impossible for the subjects of that nation in their co-responsibility, mobilized for the purpose, to evade their responsibility under any pretext of sentimentality, when no such sentimentality kept them from going to war. They have no right to soft treatment, but only to decent treatment as human beings.

INTERVENTION AND POLITICAL INDEPENDENCE

A nation has for years organized itself for war. Each successive government is a government for war. Its hymns are all war hymns. Its whole education is for war.

Should it be allowed to remain under this regime, under the pretext of preserving its independence and not being oppressed?

In the case of individual madness, men are shut up in asylums and their affairs placed in the care of administrators. If a nation is taken with a similar disease, it cannot be allowed to run riot or be left without suitable guardians.

The fact of a madman being well educated or possessing great inventive capacity is no reason for allowing him to run amok. The more educated he is, the more damage he can do. He should be kept under more rigorous surveillance.

The same is true of nations in a state of collective mysticism or superiority mania. They must be put under control as a preventive or restrictive measure.

Under political control, individual citizens will be free—far freer than in Germany under Hitler. They will be able to buy and sell, send their children to school, meet around their fireside, play in their sports grounds, walk freely about the streets, and read what newspapers they like. They will be free to hear what music they prefer, vote freely, marry whom they will, whether Aryan or Jew, worship God as they wish, or not believe in any God. They will not be kept in concentration camps.

But they will not be able to send other people to concentration camps, nor to hinder others from buying or selling, or from sending their children to the same school as their own. They will not be allowed to spy on others to betray them, or to band together to inflict beatings upon those who do not believe what they believe, or to proclaim that they belong to a nation that has been chosen to dominate the world. They will not be permitted to prepare arms to attack others, or to educate their children to attack others or even to choose governments until sufficient time has passed to make it certain that they will not choose governments to attack others.

Is this a fearful disaster?

If it is, we are sorry about it, but it would be a greater disaster if, to avoid this one, the whole world were attacked very shortly and every human being all over the world were compelled to believe in the god that was imposed upon him, in the way imposed upon him, to read newspapers and books he did not want to read, and prohibited to marry whom he would, or to work in accordance with his abilities.

QUESTIONS OF FRONTIERS AND POLITICALLY DISORGANIZED DISPUTED AREAS

In the principles that regulate possession under ordinary law there are legal provisions authorizing the sequestration of the property in the event of permanent dispute and impossibility of ascertaining who is the true owner.

Similar principles should prevail under international law.

Petty frontier frictions often provoke ill-will, and degenerate into serious conflicts; so in such cases it is better that there should be sequestration by intervention, to hold the land until a judicial decision is given.

A similar class of cases, calling for a similar solution, is that of politically disorganized regions. For many years there have been regions in Central Europe which cannot be classified as nations. Mixed populations with different traditions and concepts, grouped together in the same region, are unable to arrive at a stable situation. While one group seeks protection from one power, another appeals to another power, and finally war results.

Intervention would be a temporary solution, until complete pacification and reorganization could be achieved.

Part Two

ORGANIZATION OF THE INTERNATIONAL COMMUNITY

THE Inter-American Conference of Lawyers in Rio de Janeiro, in August, 1943, recommended :*

"That the Inter-American Association of Lawyers should support as the first aim of peace the establishment at as early a date as possible of a world organization with judicial, legislative and executive functions, based on moral and legal principles and the internal experience of all nations, and adapted to the needs and limitations of international cooperation."

This course was adopted at the Dumbarton Oaks and San Francisco conferences.

Without prejudice to what has been settled, we shall sketch out here an attempt to give efficient suggestions for a form of organization which could obtain world approval.

THE INTERNATIONAL DELIBERATIVE BODY OR ASSEMBLY

ITS COMPOSITION

RUY BARBOSA at The Hague proclaimed equality among nations as the basis of international law.

Roosevelt and Churchill, in the Atlantic Charter, which has received the support of all the United Nations, proclaimed the value of man as the basis of international law.

* The text above is the translation from the Portuguese one, the author having not had the English text for consultation.

Let us look realistically at the present world situation. Mere equality among the nations might, in the international legislative body, do violence to the desires of the greater part of the population of the world. If we bring together thirty-five small nations, we shall have a majority of nation-states in the Assembly, but representing a small minority of the people and culture of the world. Under the simple principle of equality among the nations composing the world deliberative body, their desires would prevail over those of the vast majority of educated populations of a minority composed of large nations.

This basis, therefore, does not provide a democratic solution if the numerical value of populations is taken into account. It would imply disparagement of man, whose security is the express object of international law, according to the Atlantic Charter. It would mean that an absolute minority of the peoples of the world would impose their will upon the absolute majority through the majority of nation-states, which are artificial organizations.

What is more, there would be nothing to hinder further dismemberment of the small nations. Then with each of these segments possessing a vote in the International Assembly, they would obtain a still greater artificial majority in order to prevail in the Assembly.

Direct representation of the peoples, pure and simple, would be equally unsatisfactory. Mass populations represented by misguided leaders would be able to impose on the international community desires contrary to the interests of the political organizations of the civilized world.

The two basic interests, therefore, must be brought into harmony; a legislative body must be set up on a dual basis, taking into account the representation of each state, and that of the literate majorities and minorities.

It is, therefore, suggested that:

The international deliberative body should be composed of:

(1) The nation-states through their representatives, with one vote each;

(2) proportional representation of the peoples.

The international autarchies should constitute consultative bodies of the International Assembly.

Both classes of representatives should make up a single chamber, by means of double ballot as set out below.

ITS SYSTEM OF VOTING

In the political representation of the nation-state, its people should be represented by mandate, its democratically constituted government being considered mandatory of the electoral majority through its legal representative, with a number of votes corresponding to the majority which put it into power; while representatives elected to the national assembly by the various minority parties should be considered mandatories of those minorities, with votes corresponding to the size of the minorities which put them into office.

Thus, for example, in a republic with a literate population of twenty million, four million voted and elected a president by a majority of two million. This means that three-fourths of the electorate, corresponding to three-fourths of the population, has not only elected the government to rule the nation but given it an international mandate to represent fifteen million of the citizens. The other five million will have representatives elected by the respective parties, proportionate in number to the votes they polled.

By this system the people of a nation may have one, two or more representatives, the total of whose votes correspond to the total literate population, fractions being ignored.

When there are good reasons, at the discretion of the legislative body, to suppose that minorities have not been guaranteed or that there is a false majority, the international body could sponsor a fresh election under its own control, under pain of not admitting the representative of the nation-state in question —besides other measures which may seem advisable (see under police measures and measures of security or repression and restoration).

Resolutions obtaining an absolute majority of votes in both ballots would be considered approved. In special cases a two-thirds or three-fourths majority in each ballot would be required.

If there were to occur a wide divergency between the two ballotings it would appear that the democratic organization was deficient, and an index would thus be provided of the need for taking measures of redemocratization.

We will see how the system would work:

When the official representative of the United States spoke in the Assembly his vote would be counted—one vote for the United States.

Now, if the President of the United States had come into office with the support of, say, eighteen million electors, another vote would be counted, representing the eighteen millions.

In that national poll, say, fifteen million electors had supported another party candidate while two million voted for various candidates. They would have representatives in the International Assembly in proportion to their votes and would be counted in the second ballot to complete the thirty-five million voters.

The same would happen to the Assembly mandate of the representatives of another country as populous as the United States but having a low level of literacy. Then the representative of such a state would represent the same *one vote* for his state, but only *two million* in the second ballot, proportioned to the voters who elected its President plus *one million* counted for the representatives of the defeated parties, proportionally to each.

On the other side, *one vote* of a small state would be worth the same as *one vote* of the United States. But the United States voted in the second ballot by thirty-five million literate people and the supposed small state would have no more than 800,000 votes counted for it.

We thus arrive at the following:

Majority of votes of political authorities *plus* majority of votes representative of the cultural value of mankind *equals* the will of the international community.

Would such a scheme be practicable in the present condition of international politics?

It would not seem difficult. One of the great difficulties of the San Francisco Conference was that of reconciling the political equality of nations with the actual inequality between great and small nations, and between nations of high and low cultural levels, expressed by their literacy indices.

By equal representation of states the system suggested satisfies the principle of political equality, while by proportional representation of literate populations it satisfies the two disturbing factors of the size of the populations and the degree of literacy.

The effect would be to make legitimate in world consciousness the proportional preponderance of cultured and populous nations over uneducated and sparsely settled ones while still maintaining the principle of political equality.

A necessary consequence of what is set out above is the elimination of the so-called right of *veto* which resulted in the failure of the League of Nations.

It is absolutely undemocratic that a nation with, say, five million inhabitants should impose its will on the whole world by a veto.

The right of veto is traditionally a power granted to the executive organ to avoid the excesses and collective passions of the assemblies, because of the actual contact the executive organ has with concrete problems.

It might, therefore, be preserved in the form of a veto by the executive body, unanimously or by a large majority of its members.

The International Assembly would meet annually at —————— for a period of —————— months, subject to postponement by its own decision. Extraordinary meetings would be held when convened by the executive body.

It should be the duty of the International Assembly to:

(1) Legislate on international law;

(2) Legislate on the annual budget of the international community and fix the nations' contributions in proportion to their own budgets;

(3) Decree intervention in cases not delegated for decision to the executive body, and ratify intervention exercised by the latter;

(4) Legislate on the democratic trend to be given to education;

(5) Legislate on international political economy;

(6) Legislate on the international statute;

(7) Organize its own secretariat;

(8) Create autarchic bodies;

(9) Decide on appeals from the executive body, from decisions of the juridical body as to rules for the execution of particular decisions.

THE EXECUTIVE

LET US start from a *de facto* situation—the present one. A power raised itself up to usurp liberty and disorganize the world, and other powers joined together to defend liberty and maintain order in the world.

The maintenance of order calls for reorganization.

What is the proper power to carry out this reorganization? Surely, it is that power which defended liberty and established the possibility of reorganizing—the group known as the United Nations through the Security Council it created.

This is not a right which the United Nations possess, but a duty which they have assumed by the fact of having opposed the setting up of an arbitrary order and having defended an order which would assure liberty to men and independence to the nations. If they had not assumed this responsibility they would have earned censure for not fulfilling their promises.

Humanity's right of defense places upon them the duty of establishing a democratic organization of the world and of securing its continuity. This duty makes it right for them to form an executive organ until such time as a stable organization makes it possible to see what this organ will be like in a more perfect world.

In such a case an international political fact, already existent, gives rise to a juridical fact—the structure of the organ. It seems indispensable to obtain experience of the working of such an organ; it cannot be built up in the abstract. It was the preponderance of abstract speculation by jurists, out of harmony with political needs, that resulted in the failure of both when the necessity for action by the League of Nations arose.

The executive organ in international order exercises police power, administers the activities of the superstate, and sees to it that the decisions of the Assembly and the Court are carried out.

It should be the duty of the executive organ to:

(1) See that the laws and decisions of the International Assembly are carried out;

(2) See that the decisions of the International Court are executed;

(3) Organize and superintend the sections of international activities;

(4) Organize and superintend the command of the international armed forces;

(5) Exercise intervention when the International Assembly is not in session, and, in cases of extreme urgency, even during the session of the Assembly until such cases are definitely decided by the Assembly;

(6) Submit for consideration by the Assembly the subject it thinks fit;

(7) Veto decisions of the Assembly by special majority of the members of its own council;

(8) Decree for the current year the operation of the previous budget when the Assembly fails to do so by a certain date;

(9) Solicit from the judicial organ the revision of the latter's decisions and lines of execution laid down in them;

(10) Modify the means and processes of execution determined by the judicial organ when demanded and when they are not in line with international expedience or possibilities, and submit them to the judicial power for ratification;

(11) Appeal to the legislative organ from non-ratifying decisions in the two cases above;

(12) Administer the sections of international services or delegate their administration.

POLICE POWER

The police power is based on the duty of maintaining order, securing the enforcement of fundamental principles, and preventing aggression by one nation against another.

During the initial period, when the executive body is constituted by a Security Council, there may perhaps be objections to this as illegal and to the danger of the exercise of police power which might later become a means of oppression to be used by the nations represented on the Council. Fearful of this, the San Francisco Conference gave the right of veto to the big powers.

The executive organ which has been sketched will only be effective in relation to the armed force at its disposal, and to its actual possibilities. The right of veto destroys it.

For the reconstruction of the world we should take as a starting point only what already existed, that is, some big armed nations which have disarmed an aggressor nation and will themselves remain armed until, after order and peace have been definitely re-established, there emerges to maintain order through common consent, an effective, real power, above all nations and above each of the big ones.

Until this is built up in all its power and efficiency, it is a right and a duty that those who have saved the world should remain in power. Even if there is a risk, we must choose the lesser risk. We have to choose between the more imminent danger of defeated nations or persons desiring to wreak vengeance and the more remote danger that nations which have reacted against those defeated nations and are maintaining their power would sometimes abuse this power.

There is little likelihood at present of international armed forces being formed, whether by direct recruiting or by the contributing by all nations of parts of their forces.

The police power of the international community is thus, at the moment, *in statu quo*.

But how is it to be known beforehand whether any of the component nations, when arming, will do so to strengthen the community or to strengthen itself against the community? Can one be prohibited to arm, and the rest left armed to annihilate it?

Let us get the right perspective. Compare the present world situation with that of a primitive human society in which power is being disputed by force. Either the claimant of power wins and the others become subject to him (and this would have been the case if Germany had conquered the world) or others oppose him and defeat him and become for the time being the holders of power (which is the situation of the United Nations today).

In so far as the holding of power by aggressive forces was unlawful, its holding by reactive forces becomes legitimate, until order is restored and its permanence assured. The moral fact, that aggressive force builds up to attack and reactive force to defend, makes it right for the latter to maintain itself as long as necessary.

Even leaving aside the moral fact and coming down to the simple principles of the security of all, no one would think of demanding disarmament by the defender as soon as order was re-established. Anyone who took it upon himself to do so would run the risk of being regarded as a second aggressor, and all would soon oppose him as well, with a view to preserving power in the hands of those who had shown they were capable of exercising it morally. Everyone would recognize the latter as being the most capable and worthy, and the original attitude of defending the community against the aggressor places upon them an inescapable present duty of maintaining order.

This is the real situation of the nations that took up arms to repel the aggressor and restore order to the world.

POLICE POWER AND THE JUSTICE OF THE CAUSE

A stickler for justice might object that it would not be wise to defend the attacked nation through the exercise of the police power merely because it had been attacked; that we should know first whether the aggressor is not a victim who is seeking to repair a wrong committed against him, and whether by helping the attacked we would not be siding with the wrong; and when a nation attacks another it may have a real grievance which we should not seek to smother.

Let us show the fallacy of this apparently reasonable objection.

(1) We are taking as our basis precisely the present starting point; that is, that the aggressor nations have been beaten and that a fresh aggression will not have as its cause previous aggression. If we so act from the start, from now onward the first to attack will be the wrongful aggressor. If we reason any other way, we shall be recognizing the present defeated aggressor nations as victims, with the right to retaliate.

(2) We cannot apply different principles to nations from those we apply to individuals. Though security and justice must act together, each has its turn.

What happens when a man snatches money that another is counting? We seize him by the arm and take him to the police. There he explains and proves that the victim is his debtor who refuses to pay him; yet the police return the money to the victim and jail the man who tried to collect from him by his own hands. He should have gone to court.

Very rarely does anyone assault another in order to collect a debt; as a general rule the assaulter is a thief. If in a particular case common security results in the injustice of the creditor remaining unpaid, in thousands of cases it results in the justice of protecting the owner against a thief. In the isolated case of injustice it will have been worth more to guarantee security for all, by the certainty that when assaulted they will be protected, than to do immediate justice to the man who wanted to obtain it by violence.

This illustration of an action of the local police is, we contend, entirely appplicable to international police.

However, it is not only the police who act in this way. The judicial power itself so acts, and in accordance with the law.

Here is a farmer tilling the soil. Suddenly another man, with armed companions, invades his land. The farmer rushes to the judge and requests a protective possessory order for which he gives proof of two facts only—that he is in possession and that he has suffered aggression. With this proof, the judge does not even require him to prove ownership. He grants him the possessory order and means for its execution, condemning the intruder to pay the legal costs and compensation for the damage he caused.

It matters little if the invader is the owner. If he is, he should have looked after his property; and if there was a trespass, protection would have been given him by the judge. But since the apparent situation is that the other is the possessor, the latter will be upheld even against the owner. Let the owner go before the judge to claim the recognition of his rights by means of an action of ejectment and those rights will be acknowledged. But the act of violence has to be repelled and the owner pay the costs and compensation for his violence.

This is so because in the ordinary way an invader is an intruder and the violence he does is recognizable at first blush.

It may happen that now and again injustice will be done to the true owner, but the general rule is that the occupier is the owner; and when the occupier is an intruder the owner can obtain justice without violence.

It is better to include in the repulsion of violence the various exceptional cases than to sanction it for rare cases and thus create insecurity for ordinary cases.

Our stickler for justice may here come forward again with the claim that if the International Courts fail to do justice, the aggrieved nation will be justified in maintaining its rights by violence. In this way war would be right when sustaining a righteous cause. "What other recourses can the aggrieved nation have?" asks our stickler.

In the first place it must be noted that the judge of the justice of the cause is the nation which considers itself a victim of injustice. And one who judges his own case is always a bad judge. A nation cannot escape from the rule for individuals.

The man who goes to a lawyer thinks his cause is just. If we were to let everyone who had a just cause demand justice by his own hands there would be no public security. No longer would one appeal to the powers of justice; there would constantly be crimes under pretext of justice.

The first objection to the argument is that if a nation which becomes a victim of international injustice should take justice into its own hands, the supposed justice will only be done in certain cases—when the nation that fails to obtain justice at the courts has sufficient force at its disposal. Small nations to whom injustice is done will have to suffer it.

The second objection is this. The supposed victim nation affirms that right is on its side. The victorious nation affirms the opposite. The courts have examined the case, above the interests of the parties, and attributed justice to one of them. What reason is there for accepting the supposed victim's claim that injustice has been done? For the victim is an interested party, so why should its word be accepted against that of the judges who are presumably disinterested? Why should those who have not gone into the case in detail consider the loser right when the judges who examined it scrupulously decided in favor of the other?

The third objection is that, while it may be true that the losing nation is right and the winner wrong, it may be the other way round. If the case were to undergo revision, what reason would there be to prefer the second judgment to the first?

The fourth objection is: Would it be a greater evil to suffer injustice, arising from the human possibility of error even on the part of judges, than to provoke a war under the pretext of injustice, make its own youth die by millions, carry fire and death to the enemy and run the risk of finally losing the war and thus still not obtaining justice?

ADMINISTRATION OF THE SUPERSTATE
AND ITS ACTIVITIES

The administration of the superstate should cover:

(1) Economic section: study of general economic problems and control of production and consumption;

(2) Financial section: preparation of the budget, and its regulation after it has been approved by the deliberative Assembly.

(3) Monetary section: establishment and regulation of international currency, bank or banks of issue, and relationships between national and international currencies;

(4) Military section: preparation and execution of military plans for purposes of police, security and restraint;

(5) Section for the control of factories, mineral deposits, mines and strategic materials in general;

(6) Statistical section: compilation of relevant figures for the guidance of world economy and politics;

(7) Public health section: promotion and development of eugenics and hygiene, to prevent the spreading of sicknesses and epidemics, and the regulation of the use of opiates and other drugs causing mental and moral deterioration;

(8) Education section: promotion of a higher level of education and culture, guiding them in the direction of humanity and democracy, especially by revising the teaching of history and political and philosophical concepts conducive to erroneous stresses which imperil international peace, suggesting means for preventing their propagation by any means (*note:* this section has been created by means of the UNESCO, involving the above section);

(9) Scientific and cultural section: promotion of development and coordination of culture and science;

(10) Investigation and police section: investigation of inter-

nationally harmful acts; suggestions to the superstate as to advisable measures for their prevention and restraint;

(11) Diplomatic section: approximation and harmony of the governments of the nations, mediation in conflicts; care of general archives and records;

(12) Administration section for territories belonging to the superstate;

(13) Administration section for regions subjected to police, security or restraining measures;

(14) Administration section for property of the superstate;

(15) Industrial section for industries belonging to the superstate or under its administration;

(16) Works section for the superstate and works under its administration;

(17) International communications section covering seas, rivers open to international navigation, and air; internationalized roads and international posts, telegraph and radio;

(18) Juridical section: promotion of study of international law; suggestions for legislative measures to be adopted and for measures conducive to the execution of the Court's decisions when the latter does not make them in its decisions, or for their revision when necessary through change of conditions or through their impracticability in the form determined; examination of questions submitted to it by the legislative or executive organs (*note:* this section seems to be included in the UNESCO).

All these sections are considered reciprocal collaborators in the various studies.

In the event of a nation being submitted to police, security or restraining measures, all the sections of the superstate become collaborators of the military power or of the administrative section of the respective regions.

The same applies to the administration of territories belonging to the superstate.

JUDICIAL BRANCH

WE REFRAIN from dealing with the constitution of the Supreme Court. Its structure under the League of Nations was well framed and has been kept by the United Nations; the evil was in the non-existence of compulsory jurisdiction or definite competency.

It is sufficient to state that—

(1) The judicial branch is to be the Supreme Court of International Justice;

(2) The jurisdiction of the Supreme Court of International Justice is compulsory, covering all persons recognized by international law, and there is no appeal from its decisions.

The Court's original competency lies—

(1) in matters of dispute between nations or groups of nations;

(2) in matters of dispute between persons, autarchies, nations or groups of nations and the superstate.

Recourse may be had to the Court from the decisions of national courts—

(1) when they cover matters of public international law, and the decisions deny the application of the international law invoked;

(2) when the matter complained of, or the defense, is based exclusively on international law.

It will be for the judicial branch to—

(1) organize and superintend its own secretariat;

(2) make its own procedural rules;

(3) modify the terms of execution of its judgments as requested by the executive branch, or conform such terms to the action thereon of the executive branch in cases of extreme urgency.

PROCEDURE

Under international law, lawsuits may have three stages of litigation and one administrative stage.

The stages of litigation are: (*a*) the initial stage, during which the issues are framed; (*b*) the inquiry stage, during which questions of fact are threshed out, and (*c*) the final stage, during which the case is argued and decided, and appeal is taken, argued and decided.

The administrative stage covers the execution of judgment.

The initial stage of litigation comprises the claim and the defense, and may extend to replication and surrejoinder, and the formal initial pronouncement of the judge on the issues.

The inquiry stage covers the evidence brought by the parties and that demanded by the judge.

The final stage covers the allegations by which the parties show how the evidence applies to the issues, exposition of experts' reports, and the decision; also the making and hearing of appeals, and the final decision.

The executive stage may be voluntary or compulsory, with compulsion solicited from the executive organ of the superstate and carried out by measures suggested by the Court or considered suitable by the executive of the superstate.

In each case the suit and evidence are provided by the Court.

The fundamental principles of legal procedure should be respected in all international litigation and it will be for the parties to agree as to whether the domestic procedure of one of them is to be followed, or to modify the international procedure, provided the fundamental procedural principles of international law are respected.

Should the Court not establish the details of the procedure and the parties not arrange them between themselves, the most liberal procedure established by the domestic laws of the litigant nations should prevail.

Arbitral judgment will depend for its execution on the approval of the International Court.

Appeals during the stage of litigation may be intermediate, which stay the proceeding or not, at the Court's discretion, and occur when an initial decision jeopardizes the presentation of proof or the progress of the case with probable effect on the final decision; or they may be taken to review the decision of the case.

In the administrative or executive stage, carried out by the executive branch of the superstate, recourse may be had to an appeal to the Court.

In all appeals both parties must be heard.

Whenever one party presents documents, the other must be permitted to address himself to them.

As soon as a dispute is brought to the Court, it will be entrusted to one of the judges, who will establish the procedure, preside over the evidence and report to the Court. All the other judges will familiarize themselves with the case, after which the final decision will be given. This may be preceded by oral arguments, in which the parties speak successively for the time allowed them by the reporting judge, which may be enlarged by the Court.

The decision will indicate the essential measures for its execution, but the executive organ of the superstate may apply for reconsideration of these means.

Execution is always subject to revision if there is a change in the conditions that existed at the time of the violation, or of the giving of the decision.

Whenever some fundamental alteration in circumstances takes place, the parties may apply for modification or revision of the decision to adapt it to the new circumstances. Such an application would not stay execution except by agreement between the parties or express determination of the Court.

As to costs, the regime previously established by the organization of the League of Nations could be maintained.

Part Three

EDUCATION

NECESSITY OF ACTION IN THE EDUCATIONAL SPHERE

THE great war of 1914–18 raised questions for the world which the world tried to answer during the next twenty years up to the outbreak of 1939. Here are some of them:

Did civilization prior to 1914 rest on correct foundations which ought to be consolidated, or did that profound disturbance reveal a need for rebuilding the whole edifice from its foundations?

Was the war the cause of the ruptures that then became visible, or did it merely reveal the deficiencies of the social organization that existed?

When society formulates questions such as these it wants them answered, or else it will try to answer them itself. Alternatively, it acts under the pressure of all the accumulated evil, ignorant of the fact that it does not know the dangerous laboratory where it is working.

Sadly enough, what everyone could foresee came to pass, before other and greater evil could be prevented by subjecting the causes and effects of the 1914 struggle to proper research.

In Europe, the traditional guide of Western civilization, there was mass destruction of the young men who would today be in the prime of life, forming the conservative nucleus of society. The result is a gap between the responsible elements of advanced age and the very young. The still uncalculated effects from a sociological point of view of subjecting large groups of human beings for long periods to nomadism, improvidence, the mechanizing influence of armies and often the exceeding of the limits of human resistance, have placed upon the shoulders of teachers today the task of preparing the new generations for physical and psychical resistance, and this at a time when new, greater and more startling events are taking place. Yet only so can the third and fourth quarter of the twentieth century hope to solve the greatest problem in history—that of discovering whether stability can exist on the face of the earth.

It is under actual present conditions that we have to work, live and die. We need not hope that the revolution will be complete in our time, nor is it ours to know how it will be completed. How then are we to act, if we know nothing of the end that we hope to attain?

We have to begin by organizing our instrumental knowledge —the means needed for forming fresh types of culture and the right mentality to receive it.

It would be neither honest nor human for us, knowing that we and the new generations have to go through the greatest events in history, to look, in our perplexity, for excuses—and do nothing.

If the horizons are dark, we must not say that they are inscrutable, and fail to prepare the lenses and the searchlights or to choose the highest vantage points from which we can best see into the distance.

It should be noted that we are better able to bear evils and increase the sum total of good when we do not shut ourselves up within ourselves but work cooperatively, developing a common spirit, more optimistic and therefore more efficient, which leaves less room for the anguish of considering our own smallness, the futility of individual efforts and the impossibility of doing anything really useful.

Whenever men join together for common ends, or at least make use of common means, there arises within them the feeling of collective strength, and, with it, confidence and courage to face facts.

There is no guarantee that someone with a Hitler mentality will never arise in the United States, in Britain or anywhere else. What is essential is that if he does, he shall find no response and shall end up in a lunatic asylum, a prison or as a laughingstock.

Unless world mentality is changed, what will happen is that within twenty or thirty years new generations, born during the recent war and suffering from the pernicious influence of exaggerated nationalistic ideas, political and economic levelings-out, and the intoxication of group madness, will arise, Messiah-like, with naïve plans for the salvation of the world.

What will happen then?

Another war might bring about the total destruction of the world. The atomic bomb has given us a foretaste of this, and there is no reason to believe that technical development will come to a standstill. Just as hundreds of cities and some millions of human beings were destroyed this time, in the future thousands of towns and the whole population of the world may be destroyed.

No nation has a monopoly in science and technique. It is sufficient for two peoples to prepare highly pestilential chemical products and put them into action in war to spread some uncontrollable epidemic which will cut down the whole of mankind—without a shot being fired.

Then the catchwords "living dangerously," "glorious destiny of the nation" and "national mission" will not lead their "master races" to "die gloriously" but to die miserably in the rottenness of epidemic disease.

Or, if atomic physics or explosive chemistry increases the destructive power of guns, two nations in well-balanced struggle will involve all the lands of the globe in the war operations and the result will be the destruction of mankind. A cemetery planet in ruins will then continue its course through space. inhabited by fishes and ants, a few rare quadrupeds and birds, and some miserable human survivors reduced to primitive savagery, living by hunting and fishing, to carry down the legend of a universal cataclysm which the future race, descended from them, will investigate in the buried remains of an extinct civilization.

It is for the present generation, which failed to avoid the recent catastrophe but endured humanity's most grievous event and eventually succeeded in saving a heritage of culture, to make use of the credentials its experience and hope of success provide, and prepare the mentality of the young—of those who, after we are gone, would have to endure the horrors of a future war—in order to avoid its ever happening again.

If the present generation does nothing, it will be responsible for whatever happens—for the disappearance of an age-old civilization from the face of the earth.

It is sufficient to remain with folded arms, with regard to the preparation of the coming generations, in order to commit the greatest crime mankind ever perpetrated—greater even than that of the inexperienced future statesman who might provoke a future world war.

There is every probability that the next few years will be spent in an effort to restore, and in the construction and consolidation of the international community as the supreme political entity in the world.

Yet nothing really useful or lasting will have been achieved if it is supposed that everything can be achieved by mere political deliberations among the nations or by the devotement of diplomats, administrators, jurists and politicians.

Educators have an immense task before them.

What was sketched out in the first part of this book refers to principles and to an agency which should apply them. For this agency to be efficient and able to apply the principles properly, it must be supported by an international conscience that shall protect it and recognize the rightness of applying these principles.

International law will not be able to subsist without the support of public conscience. Could the constitution of Switzerland be applied to the territory of Timbuktu?

What will be the use of organizing an international community to secure minimum rights for free men if education is allowed to take the lines of a philosophy to breed hatred among nations and destroy those rights?

It would be impossible if, within the nations responsible for the existence of the international community, contrary ideals were aroused in the national conscience when the community's action became necessary.

What will be the use of preparing, on the one hand, agencies to secure peace if, on the other hand, education is to set about to make it impossible for them to work?

The formation of this consciousness can only be achieved by education which believes in international law. There is no value in education which limits itself to propagating abstract principles.

FIXING TRUE VALUES

As a rule the human mind does not apprehend immediately the significance and the true cause of complex facts which, like war, take place partly in the subconsciousness of nations and are partly kept hidden by the governments and chancelleries. The people accept as the actual causes those which the interested parties and governments attribute to them. The real causes, when they do not disappear entirely in the course of events, almost always become known after a war is over, and even so only when the real cause, which was being kept secret "for reasons of state," happens to leak out.

The same event may or may not produce war, according to

the way it is received by the people. The idea of war does not get into the consciousness of the people until they have been worked upon by those who want war; and if the national conscience has been nourished with ideas of peace and equity and kept alive by the encouragement of the spirit of criticism, it will not easily be affected by the warmongers.

It would therefore seem that the coordinated efforts of men of good will should be directed in time of peace to convincing peoples and countries that there does not exist any such truth as men predestined to rule, or privileged nations predestined to fulfill some superior mission by means of war.

Despotism in the domestic life of peoples is usually reflected disastrously in the international field; war is brought about by self-importance, ambition and the notion of predestination on the part of the despot. In democracies war is less sought, a declaration of war is more carefully weighed, and generally is only made as an acceptance of war provoked by others. If it is true that, even in a democracy, there are some people who want war, the majority are opposed to it, and the very forms of slow deliberation by congresses and parliaments are unfavorable to the rapid maneuvers that precede declarations of war.

The efforts of peace-lovers should also be directed to making clear that what are often called race incompatibilities are nothing more than temporary misunderstandings between peoples, which can be dissipated by conscious action by the better elements on each side. They should seek to make people understand that failing, imperfect, human reasoning does not always succeed in arriving at the truth, so that right may just as easily be on the other side as on our side, and that it is, therefore, necessary to examine facts dispassionately in order to recognize the claim others may have against us.

Against all this it may be said that there were many enlightened people who did not want war, but that even so the First World War broke out, and twenty years after it was over another began under the most alarming conditions it had been possible to imagine up to that time.

We do not deny the evidence; but what would be said of the planter who failed to combat a pest because he had been unable to avoid it in previous years?

And it should be noted, too, that up to the present time peace-lovers have tried to combat war not within the war-loving countries, their actual foci, but in peace-loving countries, where the effects of the pest spread.

An international civic education system should be based on a careful examination of present-day estimates of values. What is worth defending in present-day civilization, in the opinion of all men?

Replies will differ according to circumstances and occupations. A priest will say it is religion, an idealist that it is spiritual values, a military man that it is the country's honor, a jurist that it is justice; a scientist will put science in the first place; an educator, education; a philosopher, culture, and a politician, democracy. They will all be right.

But what is Man's opinion?

What is difficult is to find any agreement as to the precise definition of these values and to determine the plane on which they all may be defended, for, up to the present, wars have been waged with the same theoretical objectives on both sides.

Both armies fight to defend the honor of their countries; jurists and politicians on both sides claim that right is on their side; on both sides God is called upon to protect armies; science on both sides is placed at the service of the fighting forces; while the very totalitarian nations affirm that they are realizing true democracy.

On such terms and on the basis of such estimates of values, we shall always have wars. Abstract notions of such kinds elicit almost universal support in theory, but are interpreted practically in opposing manners. This is as good as saying that no agreement exists as to the judgment of values, which has consequently always produced wars.

But what is Man's opinion and feeling?

Are there any values which command equal judgments on the part of all men, and which can, therefore, produce a universal agreement which would avoid wars? If there are, international civic education must be based on them.

Let us examine man as an individual and try to bring his subconsciousness to the surface, above the coverings expressed in phrases like "Deutschland über alles," "living dangerously," "Honor is washed with blood," "Lebensraum," "Shed blood fertilizes vital energies," and "War is the propeller of progress."

Let us take man's inmost self—beneath all his prejudices—where he cannot help being sincere.

The chemist in search of a new and more powerful explosive, when he is asked if he does not fear that his children may be attacked, killed, taken prisoner, tortured, persecuted by their enemies, will say that it is to prevent this that he is working for his country.

The submarine commander who destroys a liner and has his own son at the fighting front will say that he is doing nothing inhuman, because he is defending the life, security, welfare, liberty and beliefs of his fellow countrymen. He will suffer if his son dies in the war, but he will bless his death because it helped save the lives, security, welfare, liberty and beliefs of his grandchildren.

The national leader who provokes the war will say that, if he did not, the enemy nation would have time to prepare to attack and destroy the valuable possessions of the citizens of his country.

The workman will say, very simply and without any concealment: "I want bread, clothes and shelter; I want peace and security, and I don't want to be persecuted for thinking as I do."

The dying soldier thinking of his infancy and his loved ones will remember the familiar scenes, his sweetheart, and the mealtime conversations.

And if it be true that Mussolini, that consummate actor, died crying, "I gave you an empire and will give you another," it is also true that when Goebbels, the psychologist of the masses, made his last proclamation to the German people he made no further reference to "world domination," "hatred of the Jews," "Lebensraum" or "resistance to enable us to use new arms which will give us the final victory." He tried purely and simply to inspire terror of the "Bolshevist hordes," in order to strike the deepest chords of the German people, stirring them to defense of their homes, their wives and their children.

Hitler, too, proclaiming the degeneration of non-warlike peoples, inconsistently promised Germany a millennium of peace under the New Order as a reward for their war effort.

But with one accord soldiers, politicians, laborers, all people in their highest moments acclaim some very modest, simple, decent things as mankind's best possessions: security and tranquillity (freedom from fear); protection against pauperism (freedom from want); confidence that they will not be persecuted for their opinions (freedom of speech) nor compelled to accept beliefs contrary to their conscience (freedom of worship).

That is what Man thinks and wants, and will constitute a Bill of Rights.

Is patriotism incompatible with the greater development of these values, by means of international civic education?

Yes, it is, if patriotism means teaching, openly or secretly, that for these things to exist here they must be destroyed yonder; but it is not, if it means teaching that the homeland is to be loved because it secures them for us, and that similar security in other people's homelands helps to add to our own security and tranquillity, to reduce want and assure liberty of speech and worship in our own land.

Men who desire war know that one of the many factors they lay hands on in order to let war loose on the world is the formation of public opinion in favor of their intentions, for they cannot openly confess the true reasons—vanity, moral turpitude, lust for glory, or ambition to consolidate their own personal power.

And as war cannot be waged without the backing of the nation, because war is not waged by merely being declared and by armies being sent to the fields of battle, it is indispensable for those who provoke it to create and develop in the people who are to be sent to war a conviction that they are going to fight for noble, superior or, at least, fatalistic reasons. Hence the number of wars of ambition and conquest which are presented as being waged to redress wrongs or to fulfill destiny or a higher mission.

Such concepts are instilled into peoples by a slow but efficient process in such a way that at the moment of declaring hostilities it is no longer possible to withdraw adroitly without sacrificing national dignity. At such a moment war can no longer be avoided; it is too late to fight against it.

Peace must be worked for in the same way—slowly and steadily—while war is not waiting just around the corner with a people prepared for it with false ideas of justice or historical fatality. The public conscience must be permeated with the ideal of peace before the place this ideal should occupy in men's hearts has been taken by false sentiments of the justice or fatality of war.

Long before the time comes when we shall be saying, "Right is on our side," and "God is with us," we must ventilate and enlighten our spirit sufficiently to know that when war is declared the same phrases will be repeated on both sides.

Now such a spirit of criticism, enabling people to see things as they really are and not as they are displayed to us, can only exist so long as we ourselves are not involved in the bellicosity of the mass. It can develop only so long as the critical faculty finds a sufficient basis in sentiment; so long as we are enjoying peace without risk of an imminent war we can analyze with a cool head the motives that lead to war. Up to that point the collective conscience that wants peace is in a condition to listen to the voice of reason, and in so doing strengthen itself in the sentiment of peace.

If, on the other hand, we neglect to imbue public conscience with reasonable motives for maintaining peace and fail to implant an aversion for solving difficulties by violence, that conscience will easily absorb carefully administered warmongering dope, and then all work for peace will be in vain.

To work for peace can only be fruitful when it is done at the right time—during peacetime before each man is aroused and inspired with the sentiment of identification of his own personality with that of the government interested in provoking war.

All people can distinguish, in theory, between right and wrong. If asked, they can say if a general class of actions is right or wrong. But when they are asked if a specific act, done under specified circumstances, is right or wrong, some will say it is right, others that it is wrong, and yet others will be dubious.

Hence the need for education to consider concrete facts and discuss the good or harm they involve. If international education fails to do that it will remain in a Utopian world.

THE WAR PSYCHOSIS

WILL it be sufficient for education to modify judgments of value? Will that avoid war psychosis?

It will certainly not be enough just to substitute mere intellectual content for the emotional content of previous education.

The place of emotional content can only be taken by other emotional content.

The war psychosis is for each individual the expression of long-standing repression. To avoid it, something more is required than mere exaltation of moral values that are worth defending, or the determination to defend them, or a preventive and repressive juridical organization capable of intimidation. What is essential, if periodical outbursts of war are to be avoided, is an educational system which does not rely on repression but provides opportunities of sublimation.

The superior man usually preserves the spirit of initiative within his own activities. He finds opportunities for command or for making himself outstanding and obtaining the respect of others, either in the realm of science or in that of culture.

The average man also desires such opportunities, and may find them if education, developing his initiative—even though it be in the smallest things—provides him with opportunities to excel which he would not find otherwise. An accountant keeps his books up to date without a word of applause from his chief, who looks over the balance sheet and automatically initials it. But he finds extreme pleasure at the week end in showing his friend a crossbreed in his fowl run, his ability on the guitar, or a little piece of cabinetmaking with which he has decorated his son's room.

Why should not such abilities, which are so comforting to our poor vanity, be encouraged, as much as possible, by education? Why should not such factors be made use of constructively, or at least led into innocent channels?

What is needed, therefore, is a complete work of education to create opportunity for innocent pleasures for each individual. Without them the suppression that results from the monotony of life will produce excellent material for explosions at the first provocation.

So far we have been considering manual work in schools from a double point of view—how to enable the child, as a child, to let off his superfluous steam, and how to prepare him for future choice of a craft.

There is, however, a third aspect to add—that of giving every man opportunity to find refuge in hobbies, at any time in his life, from the monotony of ordinary life, to become enthusiastic and to earn respect or admiration for his capacity and so decrease the possibility of becoming enthusiastic over harmful things.

The organizer of labor is forced to consider the equation: man *plus* instrument *equals* working unit.

In view of the need for intensive production in the widest sense this equation represents a fact, whether in factory, business or civil service. For eight hours a day a man is merely an element in the equation. The working unit receives double motive force—wages for the man, and electricity, steam, gasoline, crude oil or other propulsion for the instrument of work. After eight hours propulsion ceases and the working unit comes to rest. But both the man and the machine continue to be mere elements in the equation of the working unit in repose, ready to be set in movement again after another sixteen hours. The machine stops, the man suffers tedium.

What should occur is that as soon as the unit comes to rest the man should cease to be an element of the equation and become physiologically and psychologically a man, with yearnings and interests, anxieties and aspirations. From this point of view he ought not to go on constituting an economic utility during the remaining sixteen hours. He is a moral, intellectual, emotional and social being that counts. He is a man.

Now this aspect has been largely overlooked, or at any rate the problem it presents has not been solved. The proof is that society is suffering profoundly from the repression borne by human beings who continue to be mere elements in the production equation.

THE PLACE OF EDUCATION

EDUCATION is a collection of habits—habits of thought and habits of action.

In the problems we are studying we have tried to give a truly democratic meaning to the thought of peoples, which may serve as a mainstay to the international community. We have tried to remove some of the objections which hinder the welding together of consciences in the rising concept of international law, and encourage new modes of thought.

After the First World War, all that was done in the way of education was to preach pacifism to the winner, non-warlike nations. The result of this pacifism was to destroy the desire to defend the peace.

What needs to be done, so far as the victors are concerned, is the precise opposite—democratic peace must be shown at its true value, democratic ideals must be made noble, and in particular, a world conscience determined to defend them must be created.

As regards the children and youth of the defeated countries the problem may be stated as that of removing opportunities to think and act antidemocratically, and of creating new opportunities to think and act democratically, in accordance with the international conscience.

Let the "national heroes" who were international scourges be done away with, and their place taken by the heroes of science, the thinkers, the benefactors of mankind.

Army training should give place to physical training as a basis for moral balance.

National monuments, statues and pictures of battles should be replaced by works dedicated to the modest arts of peace, commerce and industry.

The aggrandizement of combat must give way to the aggrandizement of work, effort and healthy joy.

Pasteur, Roux, Koch must take the place of Frederick the Great.

Let the legends of the simple countryfolk be sung, exalting the love of the land, instead of hymns exalting the love of the fray.

Let the weal and rest that come from peace without oppression be felt—where each man works for food, clothing, shelter and happiness, secure that honest thought will not bring accusation, persecution or disaster.

Let moral bases be established for national life, equivalent to those for individual life.

The study of the theory of the state should have at its basis the dignity of human beings, who are served by the state, the latter being a means and not an end.

Philosophy must not take the line of deifying force but that of glorifying work, human dignity, science and culture. The philosophic argument that might makes right does not make the use of force legitimate, nor does it exclude the moral values which force ought to serve, and which, as history shows, it does not serve in the end.

The teaching of history has been misused to intoxicate youth. Conquest for the greatness of the fatherland has been considered right, and so have any means that contributed to this end.

Cultural indices, economic development, level of comfort, peace and liberty of the people and social movements have been ignored.

The study of the French Revolution, for instance, ought to be developed along such lines as these: demonstration of the precarious state to which despotism had reduced France, depressing the proletariat to an extreme poverty, as compared with the wealth and dissolute life of the dominating classes, that brought on the excesses of the Revolution; the continuance of the excesses and the neglect of defense of the prerogatives of citizenship, which made it possible for Napoleon to usurp power; his incapacity to organize internal welfare and promotion of the fantasy of the domination of Europe, which led in turn, after military successes exploited for the benefit of his own family and those of his accomplices, to the downfall of France before the organized resistance of the attacked nations.

Children's games must be directed to the development of the sense of fair play, sportsmanship and knowing how to lose. They must be used for the letting off of steam and never for generating and superheating it.

Life must be ennobled in the beauty of its simplicity and honesty.

Art does not need to serve as an instrument of tyranny in order to have emotional content. Supreme art does not require "heroic" emotional contents. "Venus de Milo" has simple aesthetic content—beauty for beauty's sake. Michelangelo's "David" repulses the tyranny of Goliath.

Da Vinci's "Last Supper" has moral and religious content. Rembrandt's paintings exalt the simple life. Van Gogh's combat social inequalities. The "Victory of Samothrace" suggests rather a confident march toward a noble ideal than victory in the welter of battle.

The paintings of Napoleon's battles, with their heroic emotional content, are all inferior to these masterpieces.

In poetry, the lyric lines of Rupert Brooke are of greater aesthetic value than the epic verses of Rostand.

Epopee is thus not indispensable to works of art. If it were, it would be better for us to have less art and more peace in the world.

THE MEANING OF EDUCATION FOR PEACE

The danger of "pacifist" education depends on what meaning is given to this term.

It is necessary to distinguish between "pacifism" and "desire for peace."

Pacifists are people who do not want to be disturbed at any price. They may, however, be disturbed against their will.

We ought to be pacific, and disposed to fight in order to be able to continue pacific. It is the certainty each nation must have, that it cannot attack another without meeting strong opposition, which guarantees that other nation against attack.

The declaration of neutrality, of having nothing to do with other people's fights, is weakness; it is not even utilitarian, because utilitarianism itself demands that each man defend the community in order to have the right of being defended by the community.

Such an attitude is a blind one even from the utilitarian point of view, because it does not even defend utilitarians. Franco Spain—an example of neutrality in sympathy with the aggressor —would have had its territory occupied by Germany if Germany had felt the need or had the strength to occupy Gibraltar. It was not Spain's sympathetic neutrality that hindered this but rather the lack of effective force on the part of Germany. If Germany had been hindered from occupying Spain, Spanish territory would have become a theater of war and her "neutrality" would have proved of no avail to her. The same may be said of Portugal under Salazar.

Neutral Denmark did not escape invasion; neither did Norway, Luxembourg, Holland, Belgium or Greece.

Switzerland and Sweden did not become of interest to Germany for war operations. Turkey did, but Germany was unable to get at her. It was only circumstance that protected her.

So to be "pacifist" while remaining "neutral" is of little avail.

Pacifism is either collaborationism or fifth-columnism to open the doors of the country to the enemy, or else it is lack of intelligence, incapacity to foresee that it leads to worse harm than a firm determination to defend peace, even by struggle.

It was this last kind of propaganda which was made intensively within the non-aggressor nations, especially Britain and France, to the effect that to be on the watch against a nation that was becoming more and more prepared for aggression was to ask for war.

So education must be prepared to show that "wanting peace" is not the same as pacifism.

To desire peace is to practice the ideals of peace, work, freedom of opinion and belief. To be a pacifist is to be unwilling to defend these ideals.

Half a century may not be long enough to achieve such results of education. The adolescents of today are already intoxicated, and will bottle up the "humiliation of defeat" in order to let it explode when the time comes. If they cannot do that, they will at least do sabotage to the work of democratic education among their offspring and instill in them the desire for revenge. These descendants in their turn will have to be educated democratically in that unfavorable environment.

But if the democracies maintain a constant vigilance, and each generation carries forward the work begun by its predecessors, they will win. If they relax, they will perish, and, with them, human culture, which cost them so much to defend, will disappear forever.

THE SUPPOSED MERITS OF WAR

It is sometimes alleged that, in spite of its great evils, war produces useful things in such number, and gives such an impulse to progress, that, after all, perhaps the advantages are greater than the evils, if the general progress of mankind is considered; so that, even though the juridical sense be offended, mankind's supreme destinies must be considered in spite of the sacrifice involved for the generation that bears the brunt of the war.

This is a hypothetical argument that cannot be proved. No one knows what the scientists, artists and technicians who die in war would have produced if they had lived. All anyone knows is that the dictatorships that provoked war destroyed their own nations and nearly destroyed all the others.

The only justification for the argument would be the enormous development of science and technical progress during recent centuries.

But they developed first, and only afterward were they applied to war.

Euclid's geometry was not born of war, nor was the medicine of Hippocrates. Gunpowder is said to have been invented in China for industrial and amusement purposes. The mariner's compass does not appear to have been the outcome of war. Gutenberg's press did not come out of war, nor for war.

Laplace's law of universal gravity was not discovered as a result of war. Copernicus and Galileo set forth their heliocentric theory without the aid of war. Papin did not discover the steam engine in war. Newton discovered the law of gravity, but not for war purposes. James Watt perfected the application of steam by studying a boiling teakettle. Stephenson did not make his locomotive for war nor during war. It was not war that led Bartholomeu Gusmao to discover air navigation, Volta the electric pile, Galvani animal magnetism, nor Fulton the steamship.

Pasteur did not discover the cure for hydrophobia through any war, Jenner vaccination, Koch the tuberculosis bacillus, Hansen the leprosy bacillus, Curie radium, Santos-Dumont the method of navigating a dirigible, Edison the incandescent lamp and the phonograph, Nobel nitroglycerine, Marconi teletransmission, Wells anesthesia, Daguerre photography, Morse telegraphy, Bell the telephone, Lumière the cinematograph, Einstein the theory of relativity, Freud psychoanalysis.

Finlay did not discover, by means of war or for war, that yellow fever was transmitted by a mosquito.

Atomic theory was established a few years before the recent war.

Nor was the great Greek or Renaissance art nourished by war.

War has merely perfected techniques, making use of discoveries and inventions of peace. Scientific progress owes little to war, and cultural progress owes it nothing. Only perhaps in surgery and medicine is the argument admissible, and their progress has simply been to lessen war's fearful effects.

For the sake of argument, however, let us admit that war has great scientific discoveries to its credit, and then ask every father and mother, in the whole world, in all ages, if they would not prefer less technical progress rather than the loss of a son in war, or whether they are disposed to lose a son in exchange for a better refrigerator or a more powerful radio set.

Science has developed independently of war and served the ends of war, permitting the manufacture of such powerful instruments that a few hundred cities were reduced to ruins. What was possible in a few hundred will be extended to all the cities of the world.

Technical possibilities, hailed as advantages of war, will destroy the world.

THE SUPPOSED MERITS OF DICTATORSHIPS

Much has been said of the benefits of dictatorships and totalitarian regimes.

Napoleon III rebuilt Paris, opening up fine avenues in a grander scheme than any democratic government would be capable of doing. Hitler and Mussolini restored order to Germany and Italy; they built stadia, roads and monuments, and promoted education for youth and work for everybody.

It should be remembered, however, that these much-advertised benefits were not as great as they were portrayed. If the problem of employment had been satisfactorily solved in Germany and Italy, Hitler and Mussolini would not have had to keep on shouting for new territories to provide new fields of activity for their people.

Also the achievement of works of importance, physical training, education and the maintenance of order, are no monopolies of dictatorships. The United States has splendid roads, stadia and schools, and the people live in order. Sweden has fine roads and stadia, and has no illiteracy, while its athletes won excellent places at the Olympic Games in Berlin. Switzerland has order, roads and fine athletes, and the people are well nourished. Mussolini's Naples was no cleaner than democratic Switzerland's Geneva. Franco's Spain is no better than was Republican Spain.

Even if all this were denied, we would inquire if it is worth while to reduce mortality by wise measures and then increase it by war, killing off all the youth at one stroke; if it is worth while to raise the standard of life 50 per cent, and then to mutilate 60 per cent of the people by war; if it is worth while to improve nutrition thirty per cent and then undernourish a whole people; if it is worth while to produce a successful athlete, and then cut off his leg because of a war wound; if it is worth while to establish order among the people and then have it submitted to the fearful disorder of bombing, fires and invasion; if it is better to have mediocre roads which endured, or first-rate roads and wonderful monuments transformed into ruins and filled with bomb craters; if it is better to have lower wages and live, or higher wages and die.

It will be said that we are arguing about present-day Germany and Italy, but that it is possible to have non-provocative dictatorships.

We are not so sure. Dictatorships are generally set up when there is an economic crisis. They make appeals to the people, who renew their hopes and begin great works. The standard of living is improved artificially. Some wiser voices arise showing the artificiality of it, but they are shouted down with cries of: "Is it not bad faith to deny the evidence?" Repression causes dissatisfaction in a growing wave; repression is increased; some parrot cry is invented: "Down with the Jews who want to bleed the people" or "Long live the Fatherland in spite of destructive internationalism" or "We need to build an empire." These are the seeds of war and destruction.

In a democracy the periodical appeal to the voters prevents the development of aggressive theories, which take a long time to work up. Democracies make war too, but incidentally, while in dictatorships the war ideal derives from the need for preservation of the dictator's rule.

Even when a dictatorship seems beneficial and advantageous, it is, in principle, a danger to international order.

"A totalitarian leader must gather around him a group voluntarily prepared to submit to the discipline which they will have to impose by force on the rest of the people" (Hayek).

Frank H. Knight observes that the exercise of totalitarian power by benevolent men is about as likely as the exercise of the functions of a slave driver by benevolent men.

FALSE VALUES IN TOTALITARIAN PHILOSOPHIES

The argument of "moral debasement" and substitution of utilitarianism for great ideals was also used extensively by Germany and Italy in speaking of decadent nations who put pleasure above everything else, materialistic nations who put business in the first place, and in any case peoples incapable of defending higher ideals.

Yet it was proved clearly that those nations were able to defend what they regarded as high ideals.

Totalitarian philosophies contain no ideals; they serve as a cloak to ambitions with no moral basis.

"To live dangerously" is to attack defenseless peoples.

"To build up a great Fatherland" is a disguise for destroying other people's fatherlands.

"To arm to combat the enemies of the Fatherland" implies provoking other peoples who, when they defend themselves, give proof that they are enemies.

"To fight for glory" is to murder without legitimate cause.

"Heroism" without a cause is ferocity.

Life has to be glorified in the beauty of its honesty and simplicity. Is it "debasement" to organize instruction or try to attain a decent standard of living?

Of the four principles to be defended in accordance with the Atlantic Charter, two (the protection of peace and tranquillity and the right to work) are indispensable conditions for the other two (freedom of opinion and freedom of belief).

Do these ideals, therefore, constitute a "debasement," a "materialism" unworthy of superior peoples?

Is there any moral debasement in maintaining resources assured by a Bill of Rights in the International Statute? Surely not. After all, what is it that century-old tradition has established as a slogan for moving the masses?

Above all, "the defense of the homeland." But it confuses *defense* of the homeland with *aggression* against other peoples' homelands. As a consequence we have the absurdity of *defense against defense*. What the *Bill of Rights* will state as a moral principle in international law is *actual defense* of the homeland against *actual aggression* with respect to the right to work, shelter, bread, tranquillity, opinion and belief which each homeland ought to secure.

"To die for one's country" is another slogan. We have already pointed out that "dying for one's country" means "making other people die for their country." This is not a moral principle. To die for one's country is a necessary evil when that country is attacked. Even so, it is less desirable to die in war under the bomb debris that was our home, or to die pierced by the enemy bullet, than to come to a peaceful end in bed, after a life of decent work, dignified by services rendered to the homeland, dying the honorable death of those who have a clear conscience, in the tender presence of loved ones. What is moral is the protection of such a home, not the outrage which destroys it.

THE POWER OF EDUCATION

HERE IS a simple argument to show the power of international civic education and its benefits to the world:

If Hitler as a despot in embryo, outlining to his fellow workers the future of Germany, race superiority, and the glory of conquest, had heard from them arguments which outweighed his own; or

If Hitler, fanatical, mystical or mad, incapable of being reduced to elementary common sense simply by seeing it in others, could have been put in a lunatic asylum instead of finding submissive stupidity and enthusiasm on the part of the ill-educated masses; or

If Hitler, together with his first few hundred followers, had been seen to be a danger that would drag all Germany to destruction and had been stopped, even by popular force, from propagating the principles that led his country to destruction; or

If Hitler, when he assumed power in a Germany that was still weak, had been recognized, by a world educated for democracy, as a world peril, war being immediately declared on Germany;

In any of these cases, educative action would have been victorious.

A single German of good will by convincing Hitler at the earliest stage—if he was not mad—would have saved his country without knowing it.

If Hitler was mad, then a few Germans with critical minds would have had him put in a lunatic asylum, and would have saved Germany without knowing it.

A small part of the population of Germany conscious of their civic duties and danger of war for their country, repelling Hitler's first acts of violence even by means of arms, would have saved Germany.

Enlightened statesmen in the democratic nations, by declaring war on Hitler when he expressly proposed in "Mein Kampf" to attack them, would have saved the world from the 1939–45 catastrophe.

A single man in the first case, a handful of men with common sense in the second, a small part of the people conscious of the duty of defending liberty in the third, or a group of intelligent statesmen in the last—any of these, at successive moments, could have saved the world.

Lack of correct teaching, or common sense, or a sense of responsibility or direction are all problems of education.

If they had been regarded as such, in the international sphere, perhaps a world of peace today would have a better notion of how to solve calmly its economic and political problems.

Now let us reverse the argument.

Nazism found the German nation depressed by defeat in a war she herself had provoked through despising scraps of paper and through covetousness or megalomania of the Kaiser.

In the depressed state in which Germany found herself at the end of 1918 there were two ways open to her in education. She could arouse a spirit of revenge for the defeat she suffered in a war that she herself had provoked, or she could let her people see that the German depression was a consequence of her provocation, her covetousness, her megalomania, and that the ideals of a nation should be the same ideals of peace and tranquillity as those of each man in each family.

Germany took the first course and succeeded by means of educational processes in preparing an atmosphere in which sixty million beings would accept nazism. The vast work that was done, beginning at the pre-primary schools and going through to the universities, is something amazing, and serves to indicate the power of education.

So why should it be assumed that, if the second course had been followed, it would have been impossible to make use of the defeat of 1918 to imbue youth with the ideals of peace?

As a proof that education can control the outlook of nations, let us recall what happened with the victorious Allied nations in 1918. In Great Britain, France and the United States the people were educated for democracy; in Italy, for totalitarianism. And the result was that Italy became totalitarian, and the others continued democratic.

In view of such examples it is unreasonable to deny the power of educative processes and the positive results to which they can lead in the short space of twenty years.

Politicians know the value of education wielded through propaganda, well enough.

They win or lose votes in proportion to the arguments they provide voters against their own doubts and the objections raised by their opponents.

It is, therefore, indispensable for the international community to spread arguments capable of strengthening each man in his democratic convictions and converting others to them, especially arguments that refer to problems of everyday discussion.

Political propaganda is actually an educative process, in which the sympathetic electorate is sustained in its opinion by the arguments provided by the propagandists.

Whenever a voter formulates an argument for which he finds no reply, or hears an argument to which he cannot reply, his party is in danger of losing him to the other side.

The same thing will happen in the international sphere in education.

A democrat who suffers and finds no meaning for his suffering is in danger of adhering to some scheme of "messianic planning."

A democrat who finds no reply to the objections of a totalitarian is in danger of being converted to totalitarianism.

Why not protect him against desertion? Why not give him an opportunity to convert someone else to democracy? Why let him become indifferent or inactive?

ECONOMICS AND DEMOCRATIC EDUCATION

THE WORLD after 1914 tried to run contrary to the laws of political economy, closing custom houses, retarding production, organizing watertight economies and destroying demand, which was not excessive but was badly organized and distributed. This being so, it was hard to find an emotional motive for peace or for men to defend tranquillity, when while coal was wasted and sheep were killed to keep prices high, millions of pale, undernourished, shivering souls watched the merciless destruction of the meat that should have fed them and the wool and coal that should have clothed and heated them.

It is useless to replace traditional appraisals of values by others more comforting to the aspirations of the idealists, if each man has not the means of providing himself with the bare necessities of life—food, clothing and shelter. The whole of political economy is in question here.

If we are told that it is worth while to defend the right to work, with the resultant freedom from want, we need to be convinced that there is an economic organization under which work will in fact free us from want.

To international organization of labor there must be added technical education, life insurance, old age pensions, accident insurance, housing and protection for childhood and child-bearing. Closer contact between producer and consumer must also be promoted.

Pure liberalism cried for the organization of the policeman-state as the only kind of state able to bring about liberty, equal-ity and fraternity, through the elimination of state activities that are converted into political or economic oppression.

Democracy, however, founded on universal suffrage—which means free, informed voting—must create conditions of free-dom and discernment for the exercise of the vote, not only with regard to the political power but also to control the forces which may influence and subject true liberty by means of economic dependence.

No democracies have to the present failed to develop educa-tion, especially elementary education, with a view to preparing the people for the intelligent exercise of the vote. Nor have they failed to encourage technical education, with which people are assisted in bread-winning and, so, in becoming economically independent, which is essential for truly independent opinion. Nor have they failed to promote higher education, so as to pre-pare men for leading the country. Further, the democracies have not failed to care for public health and thus have avoided the decimation of their manpower by epidemics, nor have they neglected their systems of communication and transport, which, by reducing the distances between the centers of production and consumption, facilitate economic equilibrium; in both cases the result is to improve the standard of living and give men greater economic independence, which is fundamental for the exercise of liberty.

If this has been the practice of democracies, there is no justification for the theory of the policeman-state, which at home merely maintains order and administers justice, and abroad defends the nation against aggression. Democracy of this kind is oligarchy, dominated by the small educated capitalist group that happens to have overcome surrounding hostility.

True democracy, therefore, must act in every sphere in which the economic emancipation of mankind can be encouraged, within such limits as will avoid disturbing private economy, whether by overplanning or by extremes of free competition where equality of opportunity is at stake.

Such discreet but solicitous economic intervention constitutes an indirect educational process; it will avoid maladjustments, discontent, suppression and envy and, consequently, encourage the desire to defend the resources the democracies possess and enjoy, and with them the democracy that guarantees them. It makes the human heart into a fertile soil for the germination of democratic sentiments, which will hinder the appearance of the evil weed of economic planning or political totalitarianism, destroyers of liberty and civilization.

We must admit good faith on the part of men who, observing that the Victorian world fell to pieces at the beginning of this century, sought the remedy in a theoretical scheme for "planning" the building of a better world.

If we admit for argument's sake that this would be the best theoretical solution, facts have proved that the world will not agree to alienate the principles of liberty (which the "planners" would call disorder), because men find the best in an involuntarily planned world to be inferior to a world of freedom.

So even if a planned world were better than a world in "disorder," mankind has demonstrated that it is disposed to sacrifice itself in order to preserve the latter form in preference to the former.

In the conflict between the two ideals of "planning" and freedom, freedom has won, and it is clear that mankind will continue to uphold it.

As the "better" failed and a fresh attempt will probably lead to the destruction of the world in view of the reaction, thus resulting in something worse than either, it is for men of good faith to start from the assumption that the mentality of the world is not prepared for the "better." It would be madness to act in such a way as to provoke a fresh catastrophe.

Let us keep within what is possible, seeing the "better" is impossible and will remain impossible.

What is necessary is that those who are theoretical partisans of the ideal that was repulsed by force of arms should be convinced of this, so that they can cooperate in improving the ideal that won by force of arms.

Good faith compels us who believe in democracy to allow that at least some of those who are theoretically opposed to democracy are opposed in good faith.

But necessity impels us, at the fearful risk of perishing, to the duty of opposing them by force.

Let it not be objected that we want to oppose force by force.

The difference in practice between the two doctrines is this: both defend their ideals by force; but under one the result, as demonstrated by the German concentration camps, would be the denial of the right to life and dignity for others, while under the other the result is to secure the *right to life and dignity for all.*

Under a democratic regime the totalitarians by conviction can themselves live a decent life. The only restriction upon them is that they shall not attempt to destroy a regime under which *all can live,* replacing it with one under which *only totalitarians can live.*

The difference is a fundamental one.

For the time being, however, there are still nations which, having been defeated, are unconvinced by democratic ideals and are still disposed to destroy them. Obviously the work of educating these nations will be long and hard. So long as they remain unchanged the danger persists and their education must proceed along with the work of international security.

The democratic ideal to be established in the world does not consist of permission to destroy freedom. Whenever an individual appears wearing a shirt of a particular color and an armband with a particular emblem and proclaims that anyone who fails to wear the same symbols will be considered an enemy of freedom, he becomes an enemy of freedom himself, and must be deprived of freedom lest he destroy it.

Whenever a people, even in the name of freedom, sets up a "planned liberty," it becomes a danger to the world, and must be handcuffed until it gives up the idea and the other peoples of the world are sure that it has given up the idea entirely.

The following passages from Friedrich A. Hayek's "The Road to Serfdom" seem to us to make this point very clear :

"Planning and competition can be combined only by planning for competition but not by planning against competition."

"The whole system [of planning] will tend toward plebiscitarian dictatorship in which the head of the government is from time to time confirmed in his position by popular vote, but where he has all the powers at his command to make certain that the vote will go in the direction he desires.

"Planning leads to dictatorship because dictatorship is the most effective instrument of coercion and, as such, essential if central planning on a large scale is to be possible."

"Collective freedom [from the point of view of planning] is not freedom for the members of the community, but unlimited freedom for the planner to do what he likes with society."

"It is often said that political freedom is meaningless without economic freedom. This is true enough, but in a sense almost opposite from that in which the phrase is used by our planners. The economic freedom which is the prerequisite of any other freedom cannot be the freedom from economic care which the socialists promise us and which can be obtained only by relieving the individual of the power of choice; it must be the freedom of our economic activity which, with the right of choice, inevitably also carries the risk and the responsibility of that right."

"Economic security is often represented as an indispensable condition of real liberty. In a sense this is both true and important. Independence of mind or strength of character is rarely found among those who cannot be confident that they will make their way by their own effort.

"[There are] two kinds of security: . . . the certainty of a given minimum of sustenance for all, and the security of a given standard of life, or of the relative position which one person or group enjoys compared with others . . .

"There is no reason why, in a society which has reached the general level of wealth which ours has attained the first kind of security should not be guaranteed to all without endangering general freedom. . . . There can be no doubt that some minimum of food, shelter, and clothing, sufficient to preserve health . . . can be assured to everybody. . . .

"Nor is there any reason why the state should not assist the individuals in providing for those common hazards of life against which . . . few individuals can make adequate provision [and help] to organize a comprehensive scheme of social insurance . . ."

"The planning for security which has such an insidious effect on liberty is that for security of a different kind. It is planning designed to protect individuals or groups against diminutions of their incomes . . ."

"If, as has become increasingly true, in each trade in which conditions improve, the members are allowed to exclude others in order to secure to themselves the full gain in the form of higher wages or profits, those in the trades where demand has fallen have nowhere to go, and every change becomes the cause of large unemployment. There can be little doubt that it is largely a consequence of the striving for security by these means in the last decades that unemployment and thus insecurity for large sections of the population has so much increased." *

With every grant of such security to one group the insecurity of the rest necessarily increases. If you guarantee to some a fixed slice of a variable cake, the share left to the rest is bound to fluctuate proportionally more than the size of the whole. And the essential element of security which the comprehensive system offers, the great variety of opportunities, is more and more reduced.

LEBENSRAUM NOT AN ECONOMIC FACTOR

MANY WARS have arisen from false economic conceptions. Such, for instance, is the question of "Lebensraum." The problem does not exist, it is simply a slogan for provoking war.

Let us see what the dictators proclaim. "The Fatherland needs Lebensraum. Women, bear more children!" (We need space, so let us increase the number of inhabitants . . .)

* Quoted by permission of The University of Chicago Press and the *Readers' Digest.*

"No!" they say. "Bear children to die for the Fatherland!" (Oh, yes, bear more children, women, for them to die . . .)

"No!" they say. "You don't see the point; bear more children, women, for them to kill the children of the women of other countries and steal their land. The nobility and greatness of our Fatherland is promoted by murder and robbery!"

After all—it was said—we must recognize that a nation of seventy million like Germany cannot live shut in by four walls. This war was the ghastly result of the policy of the Treaty of Versailles, which took their colonies away.

Germany in 1914 had colonies, and still made war. Then the slogan was not "Lebensraum" but "Deutschland über alles."

The population of Luxembourg is as dense as that of Germany, and Luxembourg, without any colonies, never needed more space. Switzerland has no colonies; part of her territory is covered by perpetual snow. She has no seaports. And she has never asked for colonies. She is shut in between France and Germany, Austria and Italy, with no outlet to the sea; yet she has never asked for more space.

Looking at the matter now from the point of view of the man, is a Frenchman, whose country has colonies, more respectable than a Swiss, whose country has none?

Is a Swedish subject, whose country has no colonies, despised by a British subject, whose country has a colonial empire?

Is a subject of the Principality of Monaco, with its eight square miles of territory, more unhappy than a French citizen in his great country?

It is not the fact of possessing vast territories or many colonies which raises a nation in the world. Portugal has colonies, Switzerland has none. Persia is immense, Belgium tiny.

From another point of view, which has received attention especially from Pierre van Paassen, it is necessary to consider the economic question in order to show that the economic factors which ordinarily lead to war are more favorable to war industries than to ordinary industry. The promotion of international trade is favorable to peace, and many wars have arisen and may arise through erroneous ideas of customs policy.

WAR AND THE STRUGGLE FOR EXISTENCE A FALSE ANALOGY

THERE WERE those who hoped that, as soon as the war was over, conditions of tranquillity, work and liberty of thought and belief would at once set in.

They were and are doomed to disappointment. Education will have to undertake the task of convincing people that the work destroyed by this war had been built up during centuries. Five years were sufficient to destroy it, but five years will not be enough by far to restore and perfect it.

There will be mistakes; there will be unemployment; there will be injustice. But this is no reason for skepticism, much less for obstruction. Skepticism and obstruction are factors conducive to another war, and however great the mistakes, the distress and the injustice, they are nothing compared to another war, at the end of which the same problems will be there, the same attempts to find the way, the same mistakes and the same injustice—and immensely greater distress.

But it may be said that the law of war is the law of men, the form of the law of the struggle for existence which dominates all species.

We may reply the struggle for life had three aspects—against hostile nature, against other species, and within the species.

Struggle is a biological law. Life is a struggle and the cessation of struggle spells death. Careful observation of life, however, reveals that the fundamental, permanent, unending struggle is that between the species, one against another, while that within a particular species is merely accidental. A study of human species is sufficient to demonstrate this. Only in the cave-dwelling period might the struggle of man against man have seemed essential. The instinct of adapting his ways to his needs soon leads man to cooperate with other men so as to dominate the forces of nature. They grouped themselves into tribes.

Hatred between tribes originated with primitive economic conceptions, in which common organization for exploitation of their resources seemed impossible. Yet soon there appeared con-federations of tribes—nations—to perfect the conditions of the struggle. Thus it was further confirmed that man, though believing his enemy to be man, always decides in favor of the economic broadening and perfecting of his environment. He struggles in order to dominate his environment, and not from any fundamental hatred.

From feudalism to the great empires that succeeded it, the phenomenon and the conclusion have always been the same. Men belonging to opposing groups stop fighting one another when they come to consider themselves as belonging to the same group. They soon organize themselves into a community, having in view the exploitation of their resources and the possibility of aggression by other groups.

In the recurring fact of war, this seems clearly established: the constant tendency is to enlarge the social circle so as better to exploit resources and organize the life of the people living within the same environment.

What we see in this effort to unify and organize work for ordered exploitation of the riches of the earth is an intense drawing together on the part of cultured men with a view to understanding one another and working together for a new movement of common civilization.

It matters little that the instrument that can be used—science —sometimes comes to us from afar. We begin to perceive, through the dense mists, a wider horizon where someday we may arrive—a land where the earth is exploited for the common weal, instead of for the wealth of some.

We must not argue from prejudices that seek a scientific foundation in a false interpretation of the struggle for life.

Those who desire peace do not deny the struggle for life; they coordinate it. Man lives in a continuous struggle against nature; this is a struggle for life. He lives, too, in a continuous struggle against other species, now dominating them and making them serve him, now destroying them when they are harmful; this is a struggle for life. Within his own species he lives a struggle, in professional training, and in the manifold organizations, unions, societies and other cooperative groups.

It is true that struggle is the law of life. But must struggle necessarily mean destruction? Does it not cover an orderly, coordinated struggle such as that which men engage in among themselves in support of their own rights and of joint undertakings? The daily competition between men everywhere, every day on every subject—is this not struggle within the human species? And what of the struggle of the mind for victory?

To work for peace, too, is a struggle within the species, a struggle against other men, an effort to bring them to our point of view; it is a struggle for life, a profitable form of cooperative struggle for a more complete conquest of nature and the other species, and for a better life.

The skeptics will repeat, however, that so long as man exists there will be war. Probably, just as there will be individual crimes. Should we, therefore, desist from trying to prevent crime, or from repressing it when committed?

In crime, it will be argued, there is only one man or at most a few men against the whole of society. The scales are heavily weighted in favor of society; prevention and repression are, therefore, comparatively easy. In war a single nation can sometimes hold up to ransom all the others put together.

We deny this. A single nation, even with two hundred million inhabitants, has only a tenth or less of the population of the globe. Ten to one, even if the ten are weak, should win.

But will they conquer two hundred millions of well armed people?

It is precisely here that prevention comes in. Over-arming has to be combated; armaments have to be kept proportionate to defensive needs, and not allowed to become excessive. Thus, two hundred million will have arms corresponding to two hundred millions, and the rest of the world, with about two billions, will have arms proportionate to two billions. These two billions, by avoiding a concentration of arms in the two hundred millions, gain victory if they are threatened or attacked.

Incidentally the argument that so long as man exists there will be war was probably used to defend slavery, too—so long as man exists there would be slaves and slave owners. Yet, in spite of the argument, slavery no longer exists among civilized nations. Human traffic is repressed, just as the use of narcotics is.

But why affirm that war will always exist?

Are we to assume that mankind is imbecile or mad? Is modern man's moral outlook the same as the caveman's? His organic and psychic constitution is the same. If education and experience are not transmitted hereditarily, at least education reveals each man to himself and shows him what motivates human actions and what are desirable results, as also the undesirable but ascertainable ones. It enables him to foresee such results, and provides him with fresh motives for action.

Are we then to think ingenuously that an international organization can destroy the evil that is in the human heart?

Many who saw movies of the atrocities in the German concentration camps consider that cruelty is peculiar to human nature, for they also saw the unmerciful treatment of Mussolini's corpse; and so they refuse to believe that democracy can cure men of the practice of such atrocities. The democracies, in their opinion, are in a Utopian dreamland in this regard.

The reactions observed just after liberation, however, are explained by totalitarian education itself. Twenty years of an inhuman regime produce an inhuman outlook. When reaction becomes possible it reflects the causes which produced it.

As a matter of fact there always have been—and always will be—atrocities, apart from democratic or totalitarian regimes. Confessions are obtained by police by physical coercion; assassins are seized from police and lynched; while the spectacle of an execution has always a crowd of riffraff to gloat over it.

Usually, however, if the author of the atrocity himself is asked, he will admit, unless he is a monster, that it is reprehensible and that he acted under the excitement of the moment.

What appalls us in the concentration camps is the fact that the atrocities were carried out systematically, coldly, and not under momentary excitement or excesses of reaction. When that same question is now put to the men responsible for these camps, they say they only acted to carry out their duty, that the salvation of the state made it necessary, that they had to intimidate, and that only degenerate men let themselves be softened by the horror of atrocities.

An infuriated man is always violent. The democracies wish to assure, simply, that atrocities shall not be considered virtuous when they are for the benefit of a political regime.

POWER OF INTERNATIONAL COHESION

ALTRUISM and idealism will never prevail against interest. Idealism can only be followed when it coincides with interest. It is true that, according to this statement, idealism serves as a cover for interest; but it is on this foundation that the community spirit is built up, and the result corresponds to idealism itself.

This can be shown by individual attitudes in the presence of persons quarreling. Those not involved try to get away. If the fray is in a room from which they cannot escape, they hide behind the furniture. If there is no furniture, as the fight becomes fiercer they try to surround the person who is provoking it and overcome him. No one cares which side is in the right; all he seeks is safety which can be obtained only by dominating the provoker.

This is just what happens with groups of men; and is what happened recently among the nations. One nation attacked several others, one after another, in a room called the world, from which there is no escape. Some considered themselves protected by mountains, rivers, seas or fortresses, and kept out of the fight. Most of them were dragged in, in spite of these refuges. As the conflict spread, nations which realized the danger they were in entered the fight one after another to dominate the aggressor. Perhaps some of them acted under conceptions of idealism, but they certainly all did it in their own interest to defend themselves against the danger. When interest and idealism coincide, of course it is idealism which is stressed —in speeches.

What is the lesson? Just simply this—that nations should have more sense, and, when one is attacked, they should not wait for the danger to become greater before they take action one after another. They must take the same attitude as compact groups of men—students, workmen—do when a quarrel arises, seizing the provoker or aggressor immediately. The question of whether he is right or wrong is left for decision by means other than violence. In this way tranquillity is at once restored. It matters little that it be alleged that collective action was taken only as a result of weakness and fear on the part of the component individuals.

So much the better. Weakness became strength and resulted in common security—and the orators will talk about "ideals." What is wrong with that?

THE FITNESS OF THE INTERNATIONAL COMMUNITY FOR WORLD POLICE ACTION

It will be argued against the international community ideal that the historical past of the British, Americans and Russians is one of conquest and aggression, and that these conquering nations, therefore, lack moral authority for the repression of any nation that wants to make conquests.

This argument might be strengthened by mentioning Portuguese, Spanish, Belgian, French, Dutch, Italian and German conquests.

In this case any criminal might say: "I committed the crime because others have committed the same crime."

No, it will be said, conquest is always unwarranted but it is not for the other conquerors to judge the vanquished one; they have not the moral authority.

Recent facts belie the argument. Germany had colonies in 1914; she was on a basis of equality with other strong nations. She attacked them, despoiled them, and finally lost the war. The loss of her colonies formed part of her payment of reparations for the damage caused by the war. The second war cannot be justified on this pretext.

Italy had colonies. She made war on Abyssinia not for "Lebensraum"—which she did not need, because she had other colonies—but to "punish" Abyssinia. She *had attacked* Abyssinia at the end of the last century and had been beaten; she must "punish" her for having acted in legitimate self-defense. Haile Selassie must be "punished" for the "crime" of Menelik:

"You are fouling the water I am drinking in, lamb."

"How can that be, wolf, when I am drinking downstream from you?"

"If it isn't you, it was your father last year. You must pay for it."

Germany's trouble was that she came in too late in the race for colonies, it is said. That was her misfortune, for England got in much sooner, and does not want to share her colonies with Germany.

But England never feared the possession of colonies by other peoples. She does not feel herself threatened by the French colonies of Indo-China, Madagascar, Morocco or Algeria. She does not interfere with Portuguese possession of Goa, Angola or Portuguese East Africa. She does not get alarmed over the Belgian Congo, nor upset about the Dutch East Indies. She has never been perturbed because Tripoli, Somaliland and Eritrea were Italian, or because Spanish Morocco is Spanish. She was unmoved by the German colony of Kiaochow in Asia, or the Cameroons, German East Africa or German South-West Africa, until Germany, then possessing colonies, put the world in danger in 1914–18. Then she sought to fetter her.

The very mention of these German colonies shows that Germany did not get in late. Her colonies were larger than the Fatherland. What she wanted was to defeat England. She had a place under the sun; she wanted to take away other peoples' places. But, it is objected, for the United Nations to have moral authority to repel any aggressor they must never have been aggressors. Britain, France, Russia and the United States are wolves in sheep's clothing. Although England had no designs in Europe, she pillaged all the lands she wanted in other parts of the world. She dominated the sea routes and wants to dominate the world. That is the chief reason why she is against Germany; it is not a question of principles or ideals. Napoleon's France assaulted the whole of Europe and enslaved it, making and unmaking kings and handing around kingdoms for family gifts.

When someone else happens to do the same to her, she proclaims herself to be the champion of liberty and appeals to England for help.

Let us consider this. When France, exploited by the autocrat Louis XVI, decided she had had enough of him and deposed him she had the whole of Europe against her. Then she was the champion of liberty. When Napoleon appeared on the scene glorifying France by the conquest of Europe, the whole of Europe reacted, and rightly so. It reacted in the same way as it has now reacted against Germany. In the latter case reaction was justified; and it always will be.

"The United States became great at the expense of their neighbors." The United States had frontier disputes with Mexico. Finally, as the American element in the population of the disputed territory was greater than the Mexican, she paid Mexico for the territory acquired, just as she later paid Russia for Alaska.

She helped Cuba in the war against Spain, but later gave Cuba her independence. She took the Philippines from Spain, but is on the point of giving them complete independence.

Czarist Russia conquered Poland, tried to expand at the expense of Turkey, and insisted on having spheres of influence in the Balkans.

Let us examine the case. Poland, late in the eighteenth century, was divided up among Austria, Prussia and Russia. These were autocratic Austria, autocratic Prussia and *autocratic Russia*.

The Treaty of Versailles restored the independence of Poland. When, in 1939, Germany occupied half of Poland, bolshevist Russia sought to protect herself against Germany by occupying the other half. But she is already organizing a national Polish Government, so Russia has not the intention of maintaining Poland under her domination.

The autocratic Russia of the Czars tried to expand at the

expense of despotic Turkey. It was a dispute between totalitarian governments. Democratic England and France opposed Russia.

The Balkans are permanently coveted by Germany who, with Russia in view, wants to close the Bosporus and, with England in view, wants to reach Suez. Naturally, Russia took precautions.

But let it be admitted that the whole of this past is unjustifiable. The sticklers for justice denied moral authority to the British of today, the Russians of today and the French of today, to react against the German aggressors of today, because their fathers and grandfathers had their failings! "If it wasn't you it was your father." The grandchildren of the guilty would have no moral authority to repress crimes because their grandfathers committed crimes. . . .

It is alleged that the main responsibility for the war was Britain's. She helped relax the sanctions of the Treaty of Versailles, for fear of giving too much of a lead to France.

Those who argue thus are transferring to the police, whose duty it is to hold down the criminal, the direct responsibility for his crime when he manages to escape from their hands to commit a fresh crime. It is quite true that one policeman, Britain, has a certain responsibility for having relaxed guard as a precaution vis-à-vis the other policeman, France; but the main responsibility attaches to the actual criminal, not to the careless policeman.

The opposite argument is also used: It was the harshness of the Treaty of Versailles that provoked the German reaction.

It might as well be said that it was because the criminal was taken in charge that he refused to become reconciled to prison life, and so tried to assassinate the guards.

What should be said is that the criminal should have been placed in safer custody. The execution of the Treaty of Versailles was slack.

What stands out is the fact that Germany, a criminal by virtue of the first war, proclaimed that the war she had made did not constitute a crime, that she was innocent, that she ought not to be punished. Whether they believed her, or yielded to interests of another kind, those who guarded her gave her liberty.

Their mistake was this: Germany's second crime confirmed the legitimacy of Versailles, and only fails to justify the slackness with which it was executed.

The supremacy of a "great" Germany has given place to the supremacy of a group of "greats." So it all came to the same thing. . . .

In the first place it must be noted that beaten "greatness" proposed to plan the world by counting man as a number. Man is always sacrificed, the state grows always—until it disappears for lack of men.

Then it must be borne in mind that, of all branches of law, international law is in the earliest stages and its improvement is hindered by erroneous, or erroneously interpreted, principles, making it almost impossible to organize a permanent world political structure on democratic lines.

When, for instance, there is a successful democratic revolution in a nation subject to tyranny, democracy is not automatically installed. A provisional government is established, a government which is legitimate from the fact of having deposed tyranny. First it restores order, which has been upset by the revolution itself and which is a necessary condition for the setting up of democracy. Only after that is democracy organized; if it is not, the work will have been wasted.

The same applies to the international organization. Usurping Germany was defeated by some "great" nations, who are now restoring order. It will take time. While this is going on, the international community is being organized as best it can. Time will suggest the adoption of adequate means for establishing a truly democratic process for international order.

The question of the supremacy of the big powers may best be put on the following basis:

For the last years these big powers had to transform their peace industries into war industries; they had to train millions of men for military service; they had to prepare formidable navies and air forces; they had to organize themselves in such a way that any one of them today has sufficient power to dominate the world.

Yet, instead of following the way of force and imposing their joint will on the other nations, as it would be perfectly possible for them to do, they prepared, at Dumbarton Oaks in 1944, with the cooperation of the rest of the nations, to police the world. This cooperation would have been unnecessary if they wanted to institute a regime of force; they sought it in order to institute a regime of law, at the service of which will be the might they have at their disposal. Their aim is a regime of law on democratic lines, in which all nations have the vote, so as to make the use of the strength of the big powers legitimate in the service of the whole community.

It has been proved that force must be used to maintain international security. General cooperation will make this force legitimate and lend it prestige. There can, therefore, be no ground for fear that might may be used against right by the great nations, when they are putting the might they possess at the disposal of right and law, and desisting from the arbitrary use of power they do in fact possess and which they must retain for common security.

But if they did abuse their power, that would be the time for the community, in assembly, to make them realize that they were not supported in it. Then arbitrariness would have become evident, and that would have a wide moral effect. If, on the other hand, the weak nations, fearful of abuses, were to deny *a priori* the legitimacy of maintaining force in the hands of those who actually possess it, it should not be imagined that the latter would desist from it. They would keep it in spite of everything, for if they could not count on the help of the weaker nations, they would maintain their strength for their own security. In this case, the only effect of such non-support would be to leave the big nations entirely without obligation to intervene in favor of the weaker ones.

RUSSIA AND THE DEMOCRACIES

During the war the expression "the democracies" was used of the nations at war against the Axis. It may be asked: As compared with the political democracies, to which a system of liberal economy is essential, does Russia constitute a political democracy with liberal economy?

In considering Russia, we must bear in mind the transition from the undisguised autocratic regime of the early part of the century to the disguised autocratic regime (the Duma representative system) and the Soviet revolution of 1917 which set up proletarian supremacy with its various excesses. The first stage was a substitution of the proletariat for the nobility. To substitute a very numerous class for a restricted class is always a step toward democracy. Every revolution has a phase which is necessarily as despotic as the despotism it destroys. It is the organization stage, implying the destruction of contrary elements. It is also the stage of excesses. This stage, or at least its acute phase, has passed.

Under the constitution of Russia there is a representative government which actually does function. As regards the planned economic organization, it was temporarily a consequence of the same facts and policy.

To a certain extent, though, it showed the world that absolute liberal economy engendered inequalities, in spite of political equality, which had become theoretical as a result of the concentration of capital in a few hands. The economy of the liberal nations themselves began to suffer restrictions, in that the proletarian standard of living was raised and it was thought to secure economic equilibrium for the people in defense against the supremacy of the powerful.

There are thus two converging tendencies; bolshevism is receding from certain extremes, in the direction of freedom, while free trade is suffering moderate interference to restore social balance. One is marching from the left, and the other is marching to meet it from the right. Soon the only obstacle will be a few prejudices, which will have to be overcome.

In this transitional phase a problem arises from opposite sides and standpoints—that of bolshevism versus capitalism. Both sides are in search of stability and sincerity. What is essential, though, is good faith and good will.

SOME DIFFICULT CASES

In arguments as to the worth of the international community, we hear questions like these: Why do they not resolve the Polish case, a germ for future international disputes?* Is it lack of good will? Is it deliberate? Is it lust for spoils?

The history of territorial disputes in America is very different from that of Europe. In America, with few exceptions (Tacna and Arica, and the Chaco), territorial disputes have really been questions of the fixing of boundaries, which are sometimes resolved by direct understanding of a pacific character, sometimes by purchase and compensation, sometimes by arbitration, and rarely lead to war in defense of such territory with obscure boundaries.

In Europe there are almost no boundary questions, but questions of invasion to obtain fresh territories. To use a comparison from civil law, in America there are questions of land demarcation, and in Europe, of land usurpation.

* Written in May, 1945.

If Walt Disney put the geographic history of Brazil or any other South American country into animated pictures we should see a central region of a fixed color with hazy edges at certain points, gradually becoming sharp until the colors of the surrounding countries became quite distinct.

If he did the same with Polish geography for the last thousand years, we should see the Polish color extend northward, eastward, westward, southward, shrink to the left, advance to the right, draw in again, expand again, disappear altogether, reappear, disappear again and once more reappear.

The case of Poland reflects exactly what goes on in Central Europe from the Baltic to the Balkans: duchies, principalities, electorates, kingdoms and empires rise and disappear; independent nations become provinces, provinces are turned into independent nations, provinces pass from one nation to another. Finland, Lithuania, Esthonia, Latvia, Prussia, Hungary, Czechoslovakia, Yugoslavia, Albania, Serbia and Montenegro are names which sometimes indicate regions, sometimes nations; sometimes the nations correspond to the geographical situation, while at other times they do not.

Asia Minor is another region subject to similar complication.

Such situations engender interminable conflicts among the inhabitants themselves, who receive political guidance in various different directions, and appeal to other nations.

Under such conditions it is difficult to propose how the international community, with immense problems arising out of the war to solve, can provide rapid, final, satisfactory solutions to such problems.

There will be long, heated debates about them. Conflicting interests will be in evidence, and on each side principles of justice will be invoked. Those who will have to decide will have a difficult task, and it may happen that their decisions will not give satisfaction. What is essential is that such problems shall not lead to war.

MISPLACED SCRUPLES

Mankind needs to remember for the rest of history that scruples about taking steps to prevent the formation of a group to create a false doctrine led to the destruction of millions of human beings and the misery of millions more. There must be no sentimentality either as to preventing such formations or as to breaking them up.

In view of the universal disaster, let us not shed tears over the misfortune of those who die under punishment, as a result of having provoked that disaster.

In ancient times war ravaged whole populations, but in later times it came to be limited to the fighting forces. Civilian populations were evacuated from the war zones. More recently total war was proclaimed and adopted by Hitler, and consequently exercised by the United Nations as well.

Previously war was declared by the politicians and encouraged by rearguard propaganda, and its effect was the slaughter of young men.

Now it is different. Anyone who assumes the responsibility of war has to suffer it at home. A man leaves his house in the morning for work, and when he comes back he finds it reduced to ruins under which corpses are buried.

Hitler, Goebbels, Bormann and others responsible for the war paid the penalty with their lives. Whole German cities and populations responsible for the dissemination of war philosophies disappeared under ruins. The same happened in Japan.

The leaders who are responsible and did not perish are being judged.

Fear, whether of loss and death by bombardment or of trial and condemnation, will make future creators of war philosophies think before they act.

They must not hope that after having provoked war and having been beaten they deserve "honors due to the defeated."

They must not think that energy developed for evil transforms evil into good. A man who is chased by the police or the crowd after committing a crime makes it worse if he resists the police or crowd. A criminal's "heroism" is ferocity, whether he is the author of the death of one man or responsible for that of millions.

Heroism is something that presupposes a noble cause. If one of two nations in conflict has right on its side, the other has not. Heroism has to be appreciated in its relation to the nobility of the cause. There is nothing noble about fighting, but only about fighting in a noble cause. Apart from this, heroism is ferocity. But those who attack have not the right on their side.

Yet, when we speak of taking steps from now onward to avoid a relapse in the future on the part of Germany, there are those who exclaim: "What? Do you want to punish the grand-children of the present Germans for the sins of their grand-parents?"

It is not a question of punishment. Here we have a people who for a century have been nursing the dream of world domi-nation, who for a century have provoked terrible wars, who have destroyed Europe and threaten to destroy the world if allowed the means to rearm. It is a question of putting a stop to heavy industry, exploitation of war materials and the mainte-nance of an army with which they can attack. This is not pun-ishment. It is not punishment to stop a nation that attacked, and has just been defeated, from making fresh arms with which to attack again. It is not punishment; it is an elementary measure of world security. Punishment is for those who were respon-sible for the war.

If the aggressor nation, once disarmed, accepts the situation, she will be on the way to being able to live together in inter-national society without arms. But if she considers herself aggrieved because she is not allowed aggressive arms, it will be a proof that the step was right.

HISTORICAL TRENDS

In the past, all who fought tenaciously for their cause were considered heroes, whether their nation was the provoked or the provoker.

Since the war of 1914–18, when Ruy Barbosa proclaimed the non-existence of neutrality between crime and law, the idea of heroism in regard to fighting on the part of those who defend an unjust cause ceased, theoretically at least, to exist.

During the recent war this new conception spread considerably.

Defense of the homeland is noble, and he is a hero who defends his homeland. But the noble cause is that of *defending* the homeland, and a hero is he who *defends* the homeland. Now, if two countries are at war they cannot both be on the defense. One is an aggressor. If defense is noble and he who defends is a hero, aggression is not noble, nor is he a hero who carries it out, whether he gives or takes orders.

There must, therefore, be judgment of the particular cause, for both he who orders the attack and the chief perpetrators of it are authors of the crime and must be treated as such.

Thus there is responsibility both on the part of the political power and of the staff and executive commands.

Such responsibility is absolute, for the executives, in contrast with the victims of propaganda, are leaders, having in their hands the moral and material data of the propaganda. They are wielders of influence, not mere tools like the soldiers and the people.

In order to avoid easy sentimentality it is indispensable to keep always in memory the damages of war and connect them with the philosophies that caused them.

The teaching of history will help strengthen this.

Let us take a glance at Charlemagne, Charles XII, Napoleon, Wilhelm II, Mussolini and Hitler.

Charlemagne began his wars in 772, and when he died in 814 he had formed an empire that extended from the Baltic to the Ebro and from the Atlantic to the Adriatic. Twenty-nine years after his death his empire was divided into three kingdoms. Forty-five years after, they had increased to seven, and these in turn divided into the multiplicity of local sovereignties that went to make up feudalism.

Charles XII of Sweden attacked the nations of Central Europe, from the Baltic to the Balkans, and tried to form a great empire. Defeated at the Battle of Poltava, he returned to Sweden to find it in revolt and in a deplorable state. He died when attempting to regain his lost prestige at the Battle of Fredrikshald (1718).

"Nations perish often by their great men. Charles XII left Sweden exhausted, defeated and fallen to the rank of a secondary power. In his stormy career during which he did not doff the fighting uniform, and did not live away from the battlefields, he occupied himself only with the army. He was not devoid of administrative abilities and it is regrettable that his unceasing wars impeded him from employing them for the prosperity of his country." (Larousse Dictionary.)

So ended Swedish militarism.

"Napoleon overran the whole of Europe with sword in hand. According to his own words he made his eagle fly over the steeples of all the continental capitals. Well, of so many battles won, so many cities conquered, so many kingdoms held and reheld, what remained? Nothing of all that Napoleon had tried to establish, nothing of all that he thought to make durable.

"Let us carry ourselves to September, 1814. We are at the Congress of Vienna. Here are the Emperor of Russia, the King of Prussia, the Emperor of Austria, and an anonymous and confusing crowd of little kings, princes, dukes, ambassadors, generals and sages of their suites. What is that? It is a Congress. What does it do? Ask the Prince of Ligne. *It does not work, it dances* . . .

"What more could I say? Ah! I forgot; among other amusements, these gentlemen amused themselves breaking to pieces the empire of Napoleon. They did it so well that it was amid concerts, balls, masquerades and foolish joy that fell, piece by piece, that immense building which cost so much bloodshed and almost one million men killed." (Larousse Dictionary.)

Wilhelm II of Germany kept all Europe uneasy under his theatrical threats, ever since the end of the last century. In the middle of 1914, after the Crown Prince of Austria had been assassinated in Serbia, he incited Austria against Serbia and this provoked Russia to defend the latter. In order to attack France, Russia's ally, his Minister, Bethmann-Hollweg, asserted that treaties were scraps of paper; German troops invaded Belgium and dragged England into the war.

In order to break the British blockade, Germany attacked American shipping, thus involving the United States as well.

A revolution having meanwhile broken out in Russia, Germany made the Brest-Litovsk treaty of peace. This seemed to improve the desperate German military situation, but the Kaiser was deposed by an internal revolution and fled to Holland, from where he assisted in imposing the peace of Versailles on Germany, finally dying years later at Doorn when defeat in the war provoked by Hitler was on the horizon for his country.

From his dreams of conquest and the domination he exercised for four and a half years over other peoples' territories, there resulted the liberation of part of Poland, previously under

German domination, the geographical separation of eastern Prussia, the military occupation of the Ruhr by France, and the loss of all the German colonies.

Mussolini imposed himself upon the King of Italy as Prime Minister by means of a revolution in 1922. He undertook public improvements, and began preparing the nation for war by forming the Fascist party with its subsidiary organizations of military children (*Balilla*) and Fascist Youth.

When he thought himself strong enough, he declared war on Abyssinia to "punish" her for having defeated Italy in a war the latter had provoked forty years before. When in 1940 victory was smiling upon Hitler, who was invading France and threatening England, Mussolini declared war on France "that Italy might fulfill her high destiny."

The action of England and the United States took away his conquests, expelled Italy from her own conquests and invaded Sicily and continental Italy. Mussolini was deposed and taken prisoner, but fled theatrically. Finally it was in Italy, with her cities destroyed, defeated by the nations that had reacted against his megalomania, that he was taken prisoner again and shot by Italian patriots as he begged mercy on the grounds of having given them an empire.

Hitler the Austrian, regarded as a paranoiac at the end of the war in 1918, created in Germany the National Socialist Party and inspired the youth of Germany, discouraged as they were by defeat in the war Germany had provoked, with promises of world domination by the "master race." Imitating Mussolini, he organized the Hitler Children and the Hitler Youth. He incited them against the Jews, and, seizing power in 1933, began his horrible persecutions of Jews and of all political parties other than his own.

In 1938 he began, with the "Anschluss" of Austria, his series of conquests, which he called now "protection of neighbors," now "punitive expeditions," now "acts of legitimate defense," and after each of which he solemnly declared that Germany had no more territorial claims to make. One after another he dominated Austria, Czechoslovakia, Poland, Denmark, Norway, Holland, Belgium, and France, when he got the help of Italy against this country; attacked England, dominated the Balkans, Greece and North Africa. Then he attacked Russia, a vast area of which he seized. He stirred up Japan against the United States, thus obtaining a fresh adversary in the latter. Until 1942 he had nothing but victories. Then England, the United States, Russia, the French underground movement, and the other nations of the world, successively attacked by submarine warfare, gradually succeeded in dominating Germany and attacking her in her own territory, until she was finally brought to her knees.

Hitler appears to have died in a shelter under his own palace, under the enemy bombs that destroyed his capital. Of the beautiful cities of Germany, of her prosperity and industries, of her military greatness there remain but ruins, ruins, ruins.

So there disappeared, with Hitler, the dream of racial domination, and Germany as an independent nation.

If this is what has happened in the history of nations, while grave suffering resulted for those who opposed these dreams of universal conquest, a well-organized educational system must set out to demonstrate, both in politics and history, beginning with the elementary school, that the same results must happen even more surely from now onward.

EDUCATIONAL PROGRAM

Summing up:
Education should therefore cover, in the matter of mental hygiene, professional guidance and teaching;

A—As a means of fighting repressions that lead to war:

(1) Development of manual aptitudes—cabinetmaking, carpentry, mechanics, modeling in clay and plaster, etc.;

(2) Development of artistic ability—drawing, painting, sculpture, music, dramatic arts and the so-called lesser arts;

(3) Scout training favoring individual initiative;

(4) Physical education and sports, which provide individual satisfaction from exertion and victory;

(5) Vocational and professional guidance, correcting maladjustments;

(6) Sporting habits such as sailing, climbing, games of all kinds, especially in groups;

(7) Individual hobbies such as puzzle solving and stamp collecting;

(8) Contact with nature—flower and vegetable gardening, keeping domestic pets, etc.;

(9) Any and every other means of substituting, for monotony, pleasures that bring with them a sense of individual superiority.

B—As a means of fortifying men in democratic convictions: Teaching of history, politics, philosophy and art must develop criticism in a democratic direction to show:

(1) That international morality and individual morality are identical and that international law is following these lines, protecting mankind in spite of ambitions to ascendancy on the part of the government of any single nation;

(2) That by reason of this morality all men are fundamentally equal and should enjoy equal opportunities—security, right to work, freedom of opinion and belief;

(3) That equality of opportunity can exist only under democracy;

(4) That democracy exists only when there is universal suffrage, temporariness of elective office, and respect for minorities, these principles being secured by triple division of powers;

(5) That no nation can be allowed to disparage or attack another, because this is an attempt on the right of life, work, opinion and belief of the people of the nation attacked.

C—As a means of giving confidence in regard to international action:

(1) That such an attempt affects the international community to which we belong;

(2) That the international community is organized with a view to securing such values effectively, and that it can be effective only if supported by every man in every country.

This book may be kept

FOURTEEN DAYS

A fine will be charged for each day the book
is kept overtime.
